# THE CHRISTOLOGY
## OF JOHN CHRYSOSTOM

# THE CHRISTOLOGY
## OF JOHN CHRYSOSTOM

Melvin E. Lawrenz, III

Mellen University Press
Lewiston/Queenston/Lampeter

BT
198
·L39
1996

## Library of Congress Cataloging-in-Publication Data

Lawrenz, Mel.
    The christology of John Chrysostom / Melvin E. Lawrenz, III.
      p.   cm.
    Includes bibliographical references.
    ISBN 0-7734-2272-2
    1. Jesus Christ--History of Doctrines--Early church, ca, 30-600.
    2. John Chrysostom, Saint, d. 407--Contributions in Christology.
    I. Title.
    BT198.L39  1996
    232'.092--dc21                          96-36777
                                          CIP


A CIP catalog record for this book is available from the British Library.

The Edwin Mellen Press
Box 450
Lewiston, New York
USA  14092-0450

The Edwin Mellen Press
Box 67
Queenston, Ontario
CANADA  L0S 1L0

The Edwin Mellen Press, Ltd.
Lampeter, Dyfed, Wales
UNITED KINGDOM  SA48 7DY

Printed in the United States of America

# Contents

# A Chronology of the Life of John Chrysostom

| | |
|---|---|
| c. 340-54 | born in Antioch of Syria |
| c. 367 | baptism |
| c. 372-378 | monk near Antioch |
| 373 | *death of Athanasius* |
| 381 | ordained deacon by bishop Melitius of Antioch |
| 381 | *Council of Constantinople* |
| 386 | ordained priest by bishop Flavian in Antioch |
| 386 | *conversion of Augustine* |
| 387 | affair of the statues |
| c. 395 | *death of the last of the Cappadocians, Gregory of Nyssa* |
| 398 | becomes archbishop of Constantinople |
| 403 | Synod of the Oak; forced to leave Constantinople but returns |
| 404 | banished to Cucusus near Black Sea |
| 407 | dies in Comana in Pontus |

# Preface

The fourth century in the Christian East was a period of heightened theological activity, specifically directed at various understandings of the person of Christ, first as regards his relationship to God the Father, and then on the question of the relationship of the divine and human natures in Christ. While the major Christian thinkers continued to deal with Arianism in its later manifestations in the middle of the century, the first detailed speculations concerning the incarnate nature of the Son raised questions about how the genuineness and completeness of both the deity and the humanity of Christ could be maintained.

In the last two decades of the fourth century and the first of the fifth century, John Chrysostom gained widespread fame as an eloquent preacher first in Antioch, and then in Constantinople, where he would preside as bishop during the latter years of his life. He produced a great number of homilies and homiletic commentaries that show, from the perspective of a pastor and bishop, concern for the theological purity of the church. The aim of the present study is to investigate what was his christological understanding at a time when discussions on the person of Christ began to deal with the most fundamental issues.

Unless otherwise indicated, the Greek text used in the passages quoted is the latest available edition (see Selected Bibliography), and most of the English translations from the most recently available works.

I wish gratefully to acknowledge Marquette University and its course of study which culminated in this research. I am most grateful as well to the Schmitt Foundation for the fellowship that allowed me to do research and write at Cambridge University. I wish also to acknowledge Rev. Joseph T. Lienhard, S.J. for his careful guidance and instruction.

# Abbreviations

ACW ........................... *Ancient Christian Writers*, Westminster, Md.

FC .................................... *Fathers of the Church*, Washington, D. C.

Harv Th R............................................. *Harvard Theological Review*

J Eccl H...................................... *The Journal of Ecclesiastical History*

J Th St............................................ *The Journal of Theological Studies*

Lampe ......................................... Lampe, *A Patristic Greek Lexicon*

NPNF ............................ *Nicene and Post-Nicene Fathers*, reprint ed.
    Grand Rapids, Mich. 1975

PG ............... J. P. Migne, *Patrologiae Cursus Completus, Series Graeca*

R Hist Eccl............................................. *Revue d'Histoire ecclésiastique*

SC ........................................................*Sources Chrétiennes*, Paris

Scot J Th ............................................... *Scottish Journal of Theology*

Stud Patr........................ *Studia Patristica* (Papers presented to the
    International Conference on Patristic Studies, Oxford)

Th St................................................................. *Theological Studies*

Vig Chr ................................................................ *Vigiliae Christianae*

*Chapter One*

# Historical Background

## John Chrysostom—Life and Works

John Chrysostom is one of the Greek Fathers honored in the Eastern tradition as among the most respected ancient churchmen. His surname, Χρυσόστομος, "golden-mouthed," was probably applied only after his death,[1] although the reputation of his pulpit eloquence was well established even before he attained one of the highest ecclesiastical posts in the ancient East, that of archbishop of Constantinople. On account of his early popularity, there is an extraordinary amount of biographical evidence for Chrysostom.[2] Among the many biographers, Palladius provides a fuller picture than any other.[3]

Chrysostom's popularity further ensured that his own voluminous writings would be preserved. J. Quasten comments:

> Among the Greek Fathers none has left so extensive a literary legacy as Chrysostom. Moreover, he is the only one of the older

---

[1] The first record of "Chrysostom" being applied to John is by Pope Vigilius in 553.

[2] The sources include Socrates, *Hist. eccl.* 6, 2-23; 7, 25-45; Sozomen, *Hist. eccl.* 8, 2-28; and Theodoret, *Hist. eccl.* 5, 27-36 besides many other biographers and panegyrists.

[3] Palladius was the bishop of Aspuna in Galatia and about the year 408, shortly after Chrysostom's death, wrote his *Dialogus de vita S. Joannis*, ed. by A.-M. Malingrey (Paris, 1988) in defense of Chrysostom who had been quite viciously attacked by Theophilus, the patriarch of Alexandria.

Antiochenes whose writings are almost entirely preserved. They owe this preferred treatment to the personality of their author as well as to their own excellence. None of the Eastern writers has won the admiration and love of posterity to such a degree as he. The tragedy of his life caused by the extraordinary sincerity and integrity of his character served but to enhance his glory and fame. He remains the most charming of the Greek Fathers and one of the most congenial personalities of Christian antiquity.[4]

Had the imperial family had its way in the first decade of the fifth century, Chrysostom's fame would have gone with him into exile, but even during those years it was evident everywhere from Rome to North Africa to Palestine that the memory of the archbishop of Constantinople would not easily be suppressed.

---

[4] Johannes Quasten, *Patrology*, vol. 3 : *The Golden Age of Greek Patristic Literature* (Westminster, MD: Newman, 1950-64), p. 429. Frances Young has a similar evaluation: "If his style and methods of sermon construction fail to appeal to our taste, they were nevertheless the most effective method of communication in his time; it is no wonder that his great collections of exegetical sermons were carefully preserved and regularly read in the Greek-speaking church. His brilliant use of sophisticated conventions with flexibility and originality is hardly matched elsewere; nor is his remarkable grasp of the Christian message as it spoke to his own day. . . . In spite of the fact that he unavoidably speaks the language of the past and his works read as topical for an age long gone, his vivid imagery, together with his love and understanding of the Bible and of the erring hearts of men, gives his work an abiding quality and relevance. Christianity is not simply a set of disputed doctrines, but a way of life, and Chrysostom never lets this be forgotten" (*From Nicaea to Chalcedon* [Philadelphia: Fortress, 1983], pp. 158f).

## Chrysostom's Early Life and Training[5]

John was born in Antioch sometime between 344 and 354 into a Christian family of the upper class. Chrysostom spoke very little of his parents and his one older sister, never once mentioning any of their names. From the biographers we know that his father, Secundus, was an officer in the Syrian army and may have had a Latin lineage. Anthusa, Chrysostom's mother, was Greek and devoutly Christian. Chrysostom's praise for his mother parallels that of Augustine's for his own. Anthusa was widowed early and clung to her son as did Augustine's mother to him, which explains Chrysostom's delay in becoming a monk.

Chrysostom never knew any language besides Greek. He received a thorough education in his native Antioch, taking the course of study in rhetoric that would ordinarily lead to a career in law, although there is no evidence that Chrysostom himself ever entertained any other desire than that of religious vocation. He had access to one of the greatest teachers of classical culture in that day, Libanius, who was also perhaps the best orator of his time.[6] Libanius was well known for his great dislike for Christianity and, accordingly, rejoiced at the pagan revival attempted under the emperor Julian in the early 360's. Sozomen reports that when Libanius was asked on his deathbed whom he

---

[5] The standard biographical work of modern times is that of Chrysostomus Baur, *John Chrysostom and His Time*, 2 vols., trans. Sr. M. Gonzaga (London, 1959). See also the more recent biography by J. N. D. Kelly, *Golden Mouth: The Story of John Chrysostom—Ascetic, Preacher, Bishop* (London: Duckworth, 1995). Other standard biographies include: Donald Attwater, *St. John Chrysostom: Pastor and Preacher* (London: Harvill Press, 1959); W. R. W. Stephens, *Saint John Chrysostom: His Life and Times* (London, 1883); A. Moulard, *Saint Jean Chrysostome, sa vie, son œuvre* (Paris, 1949); and *Dictionnaire de Théologie Catholique*, s.v. "St. Jean Chrysostome," by G. Bardy.

[6] Libanius was probably more accomplished in the form of great oratory than its substance. Gibbon's estimation of him is less than complementary: "For the most part [the writings of Libanius] are the vain and idle compositions of an orator who cultivated the science of words" (Edward Gibbon, *The History of the Decline and Fall of the Roman Empire*, vol. 3 [London, 1887], p. 186).

would want to become his successor, he replied, "John, if the Christians had not stolen him."

Such was the position of the young John of Antioch— respected already at an early age for his understanding and application of the art of rhetoric, but living in a society that had not in the least given up on paganism. Chrysostom was still a boy when Julian became emperor, and when, in 362, Julian enacted legislation that allowed for total religious freedom, the stage was set in Antioch for long-lasting tensions between the many religious groups represented there. Besides the Christian and pagan segments of the population, there was a significant number of Jews, and a variety of other groups including the Neo-Arians and the Apollinarians.

Antioch was a great center of population set in a beautiful spot on the banks of the Orontes along a chain of limestone mountains. Emperors had endowed it with the finest of architecture, including its senate house, library, law courts, forum, palace, baths, and even lighted streets. Of its three to five hundred thousand inhabitants there were, by Chrysostom's own estimation, one hundred thousand catholic Christians. Besides the two main churches, the smaller but older Palaia, and the Great Church built by Constantine, there were no less than eight large pagan temples. The people of Antioch—much to the continual consternation of Chrysostom the preacher—loved their theatre and circus. On more than one occasion he had cause to contrast the people's almost unbounded zeal for the theatre and the games with their far less obvious interest in religious matters. Yet Chrysostom loved Antioch, often reminding its inhabitants that it was here that the name "Christian" was first used.

The religious side of Chrysostom's education began between his baptism when he was about eighteen and his becoming a monk. Meletius was bishop of Antioch at the time and took notice of the young John. The private schooling that Chrysostom received emphasized the study of theology through explanations of passages of Scripture, and along the way apologetics and speculative theology were addressed. It is probable that during this time Chrysostom was under the influence of Flavian, who eventually succeeded Meletius as Antioch's bishop, and Diodore of Tarsus. Diodore was also the teacher of Theodore of Mopsuestia, both of whom are often referred to as classical representatives of the so-called "school of Antioch," which emphasized an historical hermeneutic. It is interesting that Palladius says nothing about Diodore's role in Chrysostom's life.

Chrysostom claimed that he was drawn to the life of a monk while still a student. Probably after his mother died, Chrysostom joined the eremetic monks who used the cliffs and caves of the mountains near Antioch as their shelter. He explained his interest in the monastic life as that of a desire to avoid the hindrances and diversions which Antiochene society presented to the Christian life; and although his first literary activity consisted of three treatises in defense of monasticism,[7] he avoided the notion that the monastic life was the true Christian life. In later years in his famous treatise *On the Priesthood*, Chrysostom wrote: "If anyone should place the choice before me, as to whether I should be a good priest or a good monk, for my part I should a thousand times rather choose the first."[8]

Chrysostom subjected himself to physical rigors that permanently harmed his health, resulting in chronic problems with insomnia, abdominal difficulties, and sensitivity to cold. Finally, in the winter of 380-381 he returned to Antioch and permanently set aside the monastic life.

## Chrysostom's Ecclesiastical Career

Antioch would be the center of Chrysostom's activity for the next seventeen years, first as deacon, then priest, but not as

---

[7] He wrote a short comparison between a king and a monk (*Comparatio regis et monachi*; PG 47, 387-392), a response to opponents of monasticism (*Adversus oppugnatores vitae monasticae*; PG 47, 319-386), and a personal plea to one Theodore who had lapsed from his own monastic commitment (*Paraeneses ad Theodorum lapsum*; PG 47, 277-316).

[8] *De Sacerdote* 6, 6-7.

bishop. The inevitability of his succeeding Flavian as bishop of Antioch was altered only because he became archbishop of Constantinople first. Antioch had been from earliest times a major center of Christian activity. In Chrysostom's day the Patriarchate of Antioch encompassed one hundred and fifty bishoprics in fifteen ecclesiastical provinces. The church of Antioch to which Chrysostom returned, however, had for some time been seriously divided.

The effects of the Arian controversy were clearly evident in Antioch. During the days of Constantine the Nicaean bishop of Antioch, Eustathius, had been exiled. Because his successors were far less committed to Nicaea, a schism occurred two years later when a strongly Nicaean segment of the church of Antioch broke away from the semi-Arian bishop Euphronius. This minority group gathered around the priest Paulinus while the majority of the church of Antioch remained under the jurisdiction of Euphronius. The Nicaeans who remained did retain something of an identity of their own, however, for years gathering for worship in the martyria outside the city. In 360 there was a new bishop of Antioch who was orthodox—Meletius—who twenty years later ordained Chrysostom a deacon. Nevertheless, the Paulinians remained separated. The schism was prolonged by the decision of an Alexandrian synod in 362 over which Athanasius presided to recognize Paulinus, not Meletius, as the orthodox bishop of Antioch. But finally under the emperor Theodosius the Meletian party was officially recognized. By the time Meletius ordained Chrysostom a deacon in 381, not only had the Arian controversy produced factions in Antioch, but there were also other existing separate groups: the Apollinarians, Novatians, followers of Paul of Samosata, and others.

Meletius elevated Chrysostom from lector to deacon just before he left Antioch for the last time in 381 to attend and preside over the Council of Constantinople. Meletius died a few weeks later while at the Council. Under Meletius' successor, Flavian, Chrysostom developed into a pastor, writer, and preacher of great repute. But first, for five years, he carried out the significant role of deacon, which included managing church assets and property and caring for the poor, sick, and widowed. With a Christian population of one hundred thousand, three thousand of whom were dependents of the church, Chrysostom bore a particularly heavy burden. He produced a number of treatises during these years, mostly pastoral in nature. *Concerning Virginity*[9] is an exposition of 1 Cor. 7:38; *Against the Syneisaktai*[10] (Subintroductae) addresses the somewhat scandalous practice in the fourth century of some priests, monks, or even laymen having consecrated young women living in the same household with them; and *Concerning Vainglory and the Education of Children*[11] is a denouncement of the evils of pride and luxury, and an encouragement to Christian parents to raise their children in true Christian virtues. He also wrote an apologetic work at this time, *A Demonstration to Jews and Pagans that Christ is God.*[12]

Bishop Flavian ordained Chrysostom to the priesthood in 386. We get a clear picture of Chrysostom's attitude toward this vocation in his most often studied work, *On the Priesthood.*[13] In it he gives a pastoral theology and also an explanation of why, a few years earlier, he had avoided being consecrated a bishop by fleeing to the mountains and taking up the lifestyle of the hermit. The treatise portrays the high calling of the priesthood and its

---

[9] PG 48, 533-596.

[10] PG 47, 495-532.

[11] *De inani gloria et de educandis liberis*; ed. in B. K. Exarchos, Joh. Chrysostomus, *Über Hoffart und Kindererziehung* (Munich, 1955); trans. is included in M. L. W. Laistner, *Christianity and Pagan Culture in the Later Roman Empire* (Ithaca, N.Y., 1951).

[12] *Contra Judaeos et Gentiles quod Christus sit Deus*, ed. by Norman McKendrick, "Quod Christus sit Deus of John Chrysostom" (Ph.D. dissertation, Fordham University, 1966); trans. by Paul Harkins, in *Saint John Chrysostom: Apologist*, FC, vol. 73 (Washington, D.C.: Catholic University of America Press, 1985).

[13] The work has been translated into more than twelve languages. Eng. trans. by Graham Neville, *Six Books on the Priesthood* (London: S.P.C.K., 1964); critical ed. and Fr. trans. by A.-M. Malingrey, *Sur le sacerdoce*, SC, vol. 272 (Paris, 1980).

attendant responsibilities. No one should take ordination to the priesthood lightly, and no one should seek the role of bishop for the wrong motives. Most importantly, the priest must show humility and purity in attitude and lifestyle, for his role cannot be abstracted from his life.

In his twelve years as a priest in Antioch Chrysostom produced some of his most important writings and developed the homiletical skill that endeared him to the people of Antioch and the wider Christian world.

> More than anywhere else in patristic literature, in reading the homilies of Chrysostom one feels in touch with the semi-Christian populace, so thoroughly human and alive, responsive to striking image and parable, appreciative of clever speaking and yet titillated by the unsophisticated amusements of early Byzantine city life. They are a fickle crowd, lost without leadership, easily led astray, capable of riot and arson, but also of respect and hero-worship.[14]

It would ordinarily have fallen to the bishop to be the primary preacher, but Flavian trusted Chrysostom's loyalty and recognized in him a talent that should not be restricted. Opportunities to preach came not only every Sunday, but also on the many festival days spread throughout the year. The long series of sermons delivered by Chrysostom are oftentimes difficult to date, but in all likelihood we can assign to his Antiochene period most of the extended homiletic commentaries.

One unique series of homilies, *On the Statues*,[15] was occasioned by a most disruptive progression of events in Antioch in February of 387. Following the announcement of a raise in taxes by emperor Theodosius a rebellious mob spontaneously developed in the city which in a few hours time created considerable havoc. During the riot the statues of the emperor and his family had been torn from

---

[14] Frances Young, *From Nicaea to Chalcedon*, p. 154.

[15] *Homiliae 21 de statuis ad populum Antiochenum* (PG 49, 15-222), trans. by C. Marriott, revised by W. R. W. Stephens and reprinted in NPNF, 1st ser., vol. 9, pp. 317-489.

their pedestals and dragged through the city streets. When passions subsided the gravity of the act was evident to all, and the entire city was immobilized by the anxiety of wondering what the wrath of the emperor might mean for Antioch. While Flavian hurried to Constantinople to appeal to the emperor's mercy, and the authorities imprisoned any possible suspects, Chrysostom took advantage of the somber mood of the city to preach a series of sermons in which he both warned and comforted the large numbers of people crowding into the church. Shortly before Easter Flavian returned to Antioch with good news of the emperor's forbearance, and Chrysostom preached a triumphant sermon following which Antioch went back to being the city it always had been.

In 398 Chrysostom was made archbishop of Constantinople. How willing he was to accept the position is uncertain, but he was brought to the capital against his strong protestations. The new archbishop found himself once again in a cosmopolitan city, but one that was also characterized by the intigues of the imperial family and the corruption endemic to a place of power. He immediately began a reform, beginning with the office of the archbishop itself. To set an example, Chrysostom gave up such privileges as dinner parties, expensive wardrobes, and artwork. He sold much and gave the proceeds to the poor, which only served to insult the privileged class, who were welcome at the archbishop's palace only if they had proper intentions. Chrysostom continued to preach frequently during the six years he was in Constantinople, but the extensive demands of being the chief of the most important patriarchate in the East absorbed much of his time and energy.

## The End of Chrysostom's Career

The tragedy of this latter stage of Chrysostom's career is the controversy which swirled about him and resulted in his being sent into exile. His opposition came primarily from two different sources—the patriarch of Alexandria, Theophilus, and the

empress Eudoxia. The conflict with Eudoxia was the natural
consequence of the uncompromising moralism which characterized
Chrysostom's preaching. His persistent criticism of the
unrestrained use of power and wealth was taken by the empress
as a personal assault—which it may well have been—and thus the
imperial family would have welcomed any opportunity to have
the archbishop replaced.

That opportunity seemed conveniently at hand when open
conflict arose between Chrysostom and the patriarch of
Alexandria, Theophilus. There was already a long-standing
antipathy between Constantinople and Alexandria, and, because
of Chrysostom's independent personality, Theophilus had been
opposed to his being archbishop of Constantinople from the start.
What particularly angered Theophilus in 402, however, was that
Chrysostom gave shelter to a group of four monks, known as the
Tall Brothers, whom Theophilus was persecuting. Theophilus was
opposed to these monks from the Egyptian desert ostensibly
because of their Origenist leanings, but actually because of their
independence.[16] Theophilus launched a desperate attack against
Chrysostom, charging him with Origenism. When he judged the
moment right, Theophilus came to Constantinople, snubbed
Chrysostom by ignoring him, and settled in across the Bosphorus
near Chalcedon to organize as many opponents of Chrysostom as
he could find. Finally a list of ridiculous charges was brought
against him,[17] and he was commanded to appear before a synod
of Theophilus and thirty-six bishops (twenty-nine of whom were
Egyptian) at the country house near Chalcedon known as "The

---

[16] The hypocrisy of Theophilus' policy is evidenced by the fact that he
himself, before it became politically detrimental for him, had held Origenist views.

[17] E.g., "of slandering and belittling his clergy and imprisoning some of
them... of meeting women in compromising circumstances; of eating a lozenge in
church after holy communion, and of ministering baptism and the eucharist when
he or the recipients were not fasting; of inhospitality... of protecting pagans who
had injured Christians and of helping Origenist heretics, of unbecoming language
in his sermons (e.g. "I was beside myself with joy"), of eating in private to hide his
own gluttony" (Attwater, *St. John Chrysostom*, p. 120).

Oak." Chrysostom refused to appear at the so-called "Synod of the Oak," and was promptly deposed by it, not on the basis of any of the charges brought against him, but because of his refusal to appear. The emperor supported the decision, and Chrysostom was sentenced to exile.

Chrysostom left the city voluntarily, although popular support for him was overwhelming. After only a few days, however, the uproar over his expulsion and the fear of the empress over a mishap that she superstitiously took as a bad omen resulted in Chrysostom's triumphant return to the city's harbor amidst cheering crowds and waving torches.

His reinstatement would last only a matter of months. Chrysostom did not tone down his criticisms of the wealthy and powerful, including the imperial family, and soon his enemies were reorganizing to make another attack. Their strategy, influenced by Theophilus even though he was back in Alexandria, was not to put forth charges and depose Chrysostom again, but rather, to insist that the Synod of the Oak was still binding.[18] The plan worked. The emperor accomodated the opposition and put Chrysostom under house arrest. On Easter eve soldiers were sent into the cathedral and dispersed all of Chrysostom's followers, including forty bishops, not without bloodshed. Chrysostom sent a long letter to the pope at Rome. "It was just as if the city had been captured by an enemy," he wrote.[19]

Chrysostom was formally banished by the emperor on June 9, 404, and to prevent a riot that would almost certainly have resulted in considerable violence, he secretly surrendered himself to a military escort and left the city for the last time. When the people realized that Chrysostom had literally slipped out the back door of the cathedral and was gone, fighting broke out but

---

[18] Chrysostom's opponents made use of a canon of a synod of Antioch which said that a bishop may be reinstated only by a synod of greater importance than the one that had deposed him.

[19] *Letter to Pope Innocent*, cited by Attwater, *St. John Chrysostom*, p. 134.

was soon interrupted by a fire in the cathedral that resulted in its total ruin. Each side blamed the other for the incident.

Chrysostom's exile would last just over three years. Probably by Eudoxia's order, he was taken across the difficult terrain of Asia Minor to the small town of Cucusus in the Taurus mountains, which Chrysostom later referred to as the loneliest spot on earth. Though far removed from Constantinople, Cucusus was not totally isolated. Chrysostom was able during these three years to carry on a fairly extensive correspondence of which 238 letters are extant. He expresses in his letters his continual trust in the providence of God both for his own circumstances and for the individuals he left behind. He shows his ongoing concern for his friends and colleagues and for unfinished work such as missionary enterprises among the tribes.

The last thing Chrysostom's enemies wanted was the continuation of his influence in Antioch and elsewhere, and so, in the summer of 407 the order was given for him to be moved to an even more remote location, Comana, some 400 difficult miles distant. Chrysostom had already been weakened by the harsh climate of Cucusus, and in the end it was the journey to this last place of exile that brought about total fatigue and fever. Nonetheless, his escort forced him to continue to march and he collapsed a few miles outside the city of Comana. He was returned to the town and died a short while later.

## Chrysostom as a Catechetical Theologian

Historians and theologians have paid relatively little attention to Chrysostom in studies of fourth-century theology. This is understandable insofar as he did not present any new theories of speculative theology in any area including Christology. However, his writings and preaching do provide a very large window onto the theological landscape of the fourth century, and Chrysostom himself was not without theological concern. Quasten notes:

> He had no speculative bent nor any interest in the abstract. However, this lack of inclination for systematic presentation

does not exclude a deep understanding of difficult theological questions. Since this greatest pulpit orator of the Ancient Church bases his entire preaching on Scripture, the study of his literary bequest is of great importance for positive theology. His writings mirror the traditional faith with great fidelity and their doctrinal content must not be underestimated.[20]

Indeed Chrysostom had many occasions to address theological crises in the Eastern church. All of the major progenitors of heresies find a place in his sermons and writings at some place or other. But Chrysostom is not only of interest as a historical witness of theological tensions, but also as a major representative of the use of one type of Scriptural exegesis in the synthesis of theology.

### Sources—Homilies and Commentaries

The preservation of over seven hundred homilies is testimony to the interest that Chrysostom has aroused in every century since the fourth.[21] Hans von Campenhausen comments that Chrysostom's sermons are "probably the only ones from the whole of Greek antiquity which at least in part are still readable as Christian sermons."[22] Within his own lifetime Chrysostom became the most respected preacher in the Roman Empire. Circulation of his homilies began early enough that even his Latin speaking contemporary, Augustine, could quote him.

Chrysostom often speaks of his love of preaching and of the congregations to whom he preached: "Preaching makes me well. As soon as I open my mouth, all weariness is gone; as soon as I

---

[20] Quasten, *Patrology*, vol. 3, p. 474.

[21] Suidas in the eleventh century says of Chrysostom: "No man can count the number of his writings; only the omniscient God can do that" (*Lexicon* 117, 12, 83. Baur, *John Chrysostom*, vol. 1, p. 284).

[22] Hans von Campenhausen, *The Fathers of the Greek Church*, trans. L. A. Garrard (London: A. & C. Black, 1963), p. 157. Note also Jaroslav Pelikan's evaluation: "Chrysostom's homilies deserve a place alongside those of Augustine and Luther" (Jaroslav Pelikan, *The Preaching of John Chrysostom* [Philadelphia: Fortress, 1967], p. 28f.).

begin to teach, all fatigue is over. . . . My congregation is my crown of glory, and every single listener means more to me than all the rest of the city."[23] But just as often he displays discouragement at the task of reforming the multitudes: "My work is like that of a man who is trying to clean a piece of ground into which a muddy stream is constantly flowing."[24]

The biblical homilies and commentaries that are extant include systematic treatments of Genesis, the Psalms, Matthew, John, Acts, and all the Pauline epistles, including Hebrews, which Chrysostom assumed to be Pauline. Of all the biblical authors, it is Paul who holds Chrysostom's interest more than any other. Half of his exegetical homilies are on Paul's letters, and he took any possible opportunity to praise Paul as an example of Christian knowledge and virtue.[25]

While many of Chrysostom's occasional homilies and writings are difficult to date, there is a fair amount of unanimity among scholars on the dating of the large homiletic commentaries.[26] Within a year of becoming a priest (386) he wrote and/or preached a few homilies on Genesis and delivered at least the first half of the series against the Jews and Arians known as *On the Incomprehensible Nature of God*.[27] In the following three years he preached sixty-seven homilies on Genesis, a series on selected Psalms, his series against Judaizing Christians, seven sermons on Lazarus the poor man, and began writing a commentary on Isaiah which only reached the eighth chapter. In 390 Chrysostom wrote and delivered ninety homilies on Matthew, and soon thereafter

---

[23] *Hom. post terrae motum* (PG 50, 713-14) as cited by Baur, *John Chrysostom*, vol. 1, p. 209.

[24] Cited by Attwater, *St. John Chrysostom*, p. 77.

[25] There is also a panegyric on St. Paul, *Homiliae 7 de laudibus S. Pauli* ed. Auguste Piédagnel, SC, vol. 300 (1982).

[26] Baur includes in the consensus Tillemont, Stilting, Montfaucon, Rauschen, Schwartz, Lietzmann, and Bonsdorff.

[27] *De Incomprehensibili*, ed. A.-M Malingrey (homilies 1-5), SC, vol. 28; trans. by Paul Harkins, FC, vol. 72 (1984).

eighty-eight homilies on John. The homilies on John are shorter than the norm and consistently return to polemics against the Arians. To the remainder of his Antiochene period probably belong his homilies on Romans, 1 and 2 Corinthians, 1 and 2 Timothy, Titus, and Ephesians. Scholars have typically assigned a minority of Chrysostom's writings to his time in Constantinople on account of his considerably more complicated role during those few years. They include homilies on Colossians, Philippians, Thessalonians, and the longer series of thirty-four homilies on Hebrews.

Baur observes that while many of the homilies are clearly orations given with a great deal of spontaneity and recorded by stenographers, many others—perhaps even the majority—are written homiletic commentaries not all of which were necessarily delivered: "One must come to the surprising conclusion that Chrysostom, considering everything, must have written more than he preached."[28] Those that are primarily oratorical are revealed as such by the frequent pedestrian comments that they contain about such things as the weather of the day, a lack of attentiveness in the congregation,[29] or interruptions of applause.

Chrysostom's classical and rhetorical training is clearly evident in his homilies. His use of Attic Greek is consistent and careful. He takes liberties in rhetoric, however, that the more formal rhetoricians like Libanius would not have—it is obvious that form follows content in his preaching. Baur's comment summarizes both the rhetorical and the practical aspects:

> His eloquence was striking, above all, because of the wonderful symmetry and harmony of language, splendid richness of color, and intuitive art of building up images and comparisons, dazzling efficiency in the balancing of arguments, and

---

[28] Baur, *John Chrysostom*, vol. 1, p. 223.

[29] As, for instance, when he caught the congregation paying more attention to the lamps than to the sermon: "Please listen to me—you are not paying attention. I am talking to you about the Holy Scriptures and you are looking at the lamps and the people lighting them. It is very frivolous to be more interested in what the lamplighters are doing than in what the preacher is saying. After all, I am lighting a lamp too—the lamp of God's word" (Attwater, *St. John Chrysostom*, p. 42).

magnificent climaxes; but above all an often overpowering and involved fulness of thought, of images and tones, rich, keen and bold fantasies, an outstanding memory and brilliant facility of expression. But above all he never floated in the clouds, but stood always on the firm ground of actuality, and spoke out of the fulness of practical experience of life.[30]

The homilies themselves give a clear picture of the audiences to which Chrysostom spoke both in Antioch and Constantinople. Many were uneducated laborers and slaves—Chrysostom's frequent words of encouragement bear testimony to this; but the very wealthiest and educated came to listen at the same time. To them the preacher makes frequent appeals for fairness and generosity, and encourages them to come to the sermon having already read the biblical passage at hand.[31] We also learn of some of the peculiarities of Chrysostom's congregations, as, for instance, when he warns them to be careful of their money in church because of the number of pickpockets circulating among them;[32] or when he chastizes the congregation for their tendency to come to hear the sermon, but then leave before the Eucharist.[33]

The content of Chrysostom's preaching is clearly twofold: the dogmatic and the moral. In fact, almost all the exegetical homilies are divided into this simple two-part form. While some of his sermons could be delivered in five or ten minutes, others range upwards of one and a half hours. The norm seems to be approximately thirty to sixty minutes. The moral concerns presented center around a few favorite themes like marriage and

---

[30] Baur, *John Chrysostom*, vol. 1, p. 223.

[31] "I admonish and beg you incessantly that you not only pay attention to what is said here in the church, but also diligently read the Holy Scripture at home. Let no one come to me with that cold and altogether objectionable excuse and say, I am a lawyer, I am a city counselor, I am a laborer, I have a wife and must care for my children. . . I am a man of the world; it is not my business to read the Scriptures" (*Hom. 3 de Lazaro* 1-2 [PG 48, 991-3]).

[32] *De Incomprehensibili* 4, 445-55 (Malingrey, p. 264). English trans. by Paul Harkins, *FC*, vol. 72 (1984).

[33] Cited by Attwater, *St. John Chrysostom*, p. 42.

the family, avoidance of the circus and theatre, but especially the virtues of generosity and almsgiving.[34] But of particular interest here is the dogmatic content of his sermons. One of the primary reasons Chrysostom does address christological issues is because of the theological tensions predominant in places like Antioch and Constantinople. Arians and Neo-Arians were well represented in both places, and became especially problematic when Theodosius' closing the Arian churches resulted in the influx of many into the catholic churches. Chrysostom found himself preaching to mixed congregations and, accordingly, moved back and forth between apologetics and catechesis.

## Exegesis and Theology

Chrysostom's teachers at Antioch were inclined toward a more exegetical than speculative theology, and Chrysostom followed that tradition throughout his career.[35] His teaching consisted mostly in the systematic exegesis of Scripture out of a grammatical/historical hermeneutic which was one of the major factors influencing his Christology.

During the years he spent as a monk he had ample opportunity to memorize large sections, if not the entirety, of the New Testament.[36] All in all, Chrysostom cited the Scriptures over 18,000 times: 7,000 times the Old Testament, and 11,000 times

---

[34] See for example the seven sermons on the parable of Lazarus and the rich man, trans. by C. Roth, *On Wealth and Poverty* (Crestwood N.Y.: St. Vladimir's Seminary Press, 1984). Baur notes, for instance, the frequency with which Chrysostom returns to this theme just in the homilies on Matthew. In ninety sermons he spoke forty times on almsgiving, thirteen times on poverty, thirty times on avarice, and twenty times on wrongly acquired and wrongly used wealth. Baur, *John Chrysostom*, vol. 1, p. 215.

[35] See F. H. Chase, *Chrysostom: A Study in the History of Biblical Interpretation* (Cambridge, 1887); Peter Gorday, "The Place of Chapters 9-11 in the Argument of the Epistle to the Romans: A Study of the Romans Exegesis of Origen, John Chrysostom and Augustine" (Ph.D. dissertation, Vanderbilt University, 1980); and T. R. McKibbens, "The Exegesis of John Chrysostom: Homilies on the Gospels," *Expository Times* 93 (June 1982): 264-70.

[36] Palladius,*Vita*, 5.

the New. He showed preferences for the Psalms (1500+ occurences) and Genesis (900+) in the Old Testament; and for the gospels of Matthew (2400+) and John (1300+) and the major Pauline epistles 1 and 2 Corinthians (2100+) and Romans (900+) in the New Testament.[37] Chrysostom never learned Hebrew and was thus dependent upon Greek translations of the Old Testament. His care in exegesis is demonstrated in that he used not only the Septuagint, but the versions of Symmachus, Theodotion, and Aquila as well.

The Antiochenes consciously rejected allegorical interpretation typified by the Alexandrians, particularly Origen. Diodore, Chrysostom's teacher, had learned from his teacher, Eusebius of Emesa, a more historical hermeneutic.[38] Presumably Diodore explained his methodology in his On the Difference Between Theory and Allegory which did not survive his condemnation by a later generation. Yet the Antiochenes did not reject allegory and typology altogether. What they required was evidence from the text itself that a figurative interpretation was necessary. Chrysostom was probably less rigid in the rejection of allegory than Diodore or his fellow pupil, Theodore of Mopsuestia, in that he would occasionally use typology, especially where it would help him in apologetical discussions with Jews or Arians. Nevertheless his overall approach is generally to take the Scriptures at face value and where there is a problem of fact or morality, to use a rational argument either to harmonize the details or to uncover a deeper significance.

It is because Chrysostom ranks the truth of the Christian Scriptures far above any of the constructions of the philosophers that he at times appears opposed to the whole classical

---

[37] That, according to Baur, John Chrysostom, vol. 1, p. 316. See also R. A. Krupp, Saint John Chrysostom: A Scripture Index (Lanham, MD: University Press of America, 1984).

[38] Eduard Schweizer, "Diodor von Tarsus als Exeget," Zeitschrift für die neutestamentliche Wissenschaft 40 (1941): 33-75.

tradition.[39] It is true that he often spoke disparagingly of the "Greeks," by which, of course, he meant pagans, but it is hard to distinguish between the philosophical teachings of the pagans and the distinctly non-Christian religious systems and morality that Chrysostom most certainly was including in his rejection. But on numerous occasions he quotes Plato in a positive way, and cites such classical authors as Homer, Sophocles, and Euripides, among others. Yet he often reminds his congregation that the Christians have something none of the Greeks can claim—the revelation of the Scriptures, and that given through the uneducated apostles. One can hear in Chrysostom's criticism of pagan philosophy at one and the same time an apologetic directed at the still numerous pagan population of Antioch, a catechesis that is intended to break down barriers of social class and education, and a polemic against the pockets of cultural pride. Chrysostom was still burying Julian long after he and his attempt at pagan revival had died.

When Chrysostom is studied from a theological perspective, then, what one finds is an exegetical and cathechetical approach through which he defends the consensus reached in the East by the end of the fourth century. In most areas—theology proper, anthropology, ecclesiology, eschatology—Chrysostom is a witness to the main streams of Eastern theology, and thus is quoted with great frequency in the centuries to follow as an authoritative voice. Augustine calls him a faithful witness of Christian belief, a man who was "eruditus et erudiens" in the catholic faith, and to be ranked among the most distinguished learned men.[40] When Pelagius used Chrysostom for support of his views in his *De natura*, Augustine replied in *De natura et gratia* (415) that Pelagius had misunderstood him. And Chrysostom's views on Christology

---

[39] On Chrysostom's relationship to the classical tradition see G. J. M. Bartelink, " 'Philosophie' et 'Philosophe' dans quelques oeuvres de Jean Chrysostome," *Revue d'ascétique et de mystique* 144 (1960): 486-92; and P. R. Coleman-Norton, "St. Chrysostom and the Greek Philosophers," *Classical Philology* 25 (1930): 305-7.

[40] *Contra Julianum* 1, 6, 22. See Baur, *John Chrysostom*, vol. 1, 365.

were quoted at least once in a pivotal statement. The Council of Chalcedon used one of his statements from his homilies on John— "By their union and conjoining God, the Word, and the flesh are one, not as a result of commingling or disappearance of substances, but by some ineffable and inexplicable union"[41]—in support of its christological definition. Indeed he is aware of the meaning and importance of such terms as *ousia, physis, hypostasis, prosopon,* and *homoousios,* and he can see the issues arising in the nascent christological problem. Contained in his homilies is at least some evidence of how far the Christology of the East had developed in the generations between Nicaea and Chalcedon.

## Studies Relating to Chrysostom's Christology

Of all the theological themes that are treated by Chrysostom in his preaching and writings, the doctrine of Christ gets the most attention. There were apologetic reasons for this, insofar as the activities of Jews and pagans necessitated continuous discourse explaining the unique figure of Christ; and there were polemical reasons as well, on account of the continued presence of Arians, Manichaeans, Docetists, and other heretical groups.

The few studies that have been done of Chrysostom's Christology and the passing references he receives in histories of dogma in large part have sought to understand his views in the light of Chalcedon. Until fairly recent times it was assumed this classic Antiochene interpreter of the Scriptures reflected the classic Antiochene Christology—one that emphasizes the distinctness of the two natures in order to assure the integrity of both. One important reason for a new study on the question is that the Antioch-Alexandria paradigm has gone through significant modifications in recent scholarship. Of no less importance is the fact that some of the key texts used in past studies are no longer considered authentic. Before noting these

---

[41] *Hom. in Jn.* 11, 2 (PG 59, 80).

specific studies, however, I will summarize the antecedent history of the christological controversy.

## Background to Fourth Century Christology

The earliest Christology, that of the authors of the New Testament, depicts Christ variously as the fulfillment of messianic expectations ("Jesus," "Son of man," etc.) and the cosmic master ("Logos," "Kyrios," etc.), and determined that two key questions would inevitably be raised—what is the relationship of Christ to the Father? and, what is the relationship of the divinity and the humanity within Christ? From the earliest literature outside of the New Testament it was common to describe Christ as preexistent and, in terms of his incarnation, as a duality. So Ignatius says: "There is only one physician—of flesh yet spiritual, born yet unbegotten, God incarnate, genuine life in the midst of death, sprung from Mary as well as God, first subject to suffering then beyond it—Jesus Christ our Lord."[42]

With the Apologists of the second century comes the linkage of the Logos of John's Gospel with that of the Stoics. Justin, for example, understood Christ as that Logos which is reason itself, the reason of the cosmos, which has contact with and governs the material universe. The Logos is derived from ultimate deity and thus the Father is protected from involvement in the mutable universe. Justin saw no problem in thus depicting Christ as derived, as "numerically distinct" (καὶ ἀριθμῷ ἕτερον) but others, the monarchians, eventually reacted to the supposed threat of polytheism either by understanding the Son as one mode of the divine unity or as the adopted Son.

The Gnostics of the second and third centuries presented a distinctly different view of Christ necessitated by their assumption of a radical dualism of spirit and matter. The earthly manifestation of Christ only seemed to be a bodily incarnation, for the notion of contact of divinity with the material order was at the

---

[42] *Ephesians* 7, 2.

very least irrelevant. This docetic understanding represented in Marcion, Valentinus, Basilides, and others prompted responses from writers like Tertullian and Irenaeus that included strong affirmations of the real flesh of Christ. Just what that flesh entailed, how fully human it was, was a topic only superficially treated in the third and fourth centuries. But the Gnostics presented a further problem in that Christ as the divine redeemer was, to them, one of many emanations of the supreme divine being, and thus was seen to occupy a position in the great chain of being that is less than that of full divinity.

The same problem was true also of Justin's Logos-theology and to some degree in Origen's understanding. Origen reflected the prevailing Platonism of his native Alexandria in the soteriological presuppositions that underlie his Christology. All souls have pre-existed, and God used the one soul that did not fall away—that of Jesus—to be united with his Logos or Wisdom which in turn became united with human flesh thus providing a way of redemption for the race. This Logos, which in Christ corresponds to the soul, is eternal but derived. That is, the Logos is begotten of God and can even be called a "secondary God" (δεύτερος θεός) but is begotten eternally. As eternal the Logos possesses a status better than the creatures, but there is still a distinct subordination of the Logos to God insofar as he occupies the next rung down on the hierarchical ladder.

The Arian controversy of the early fourth century brought into boldest relief the divergence of metaphysical assumptions held by those who assigned the Son an inferior status and those who maintained the fully equal status of Son with the Father. In the year 318 a presbyter of Alexandria named Arius drew the bishop, Alexander, into open controversy by his clear assertion of the creaturely status of the Son. Arius' intention was to maintain the transcendence of God and the mediatorial position of the Logos.[43]

---

[43] One study of early Arianism attempts to demonstrate that it is not simply the consequence of metaphysical assumptions about the nature of deity, but that it

But it would not eventually prove satisfying to the majority to call the Son divine to a lesser degree than the Father and to deny the truly eternal existence of the Son by saying that "there was a time when he was not."

Athanasius, bishop of Alexandria, insisted on the full divinity of the Son for a soteriological reason. Because human beings were made in the image of God they are partakers of the divine nature. Their fallenness is a corruption of their created "divine" nature, and redemption could occur only if God himself reconstituted that nature. Thus, the incarnation of the fully divine Son was not an impossibility; indeed, it was a necessity. To keep the Logos one step removed from full divinity (as did the Arians) or one step removed from real flesh (as did the Docetists) would, in Athanasius' opinion, nullify the whole redemptive purpose and the efficacy of the incarnation.

Though their understanding of the Logos differed radically, both the Arians and Athanasius saw no real necessity to affirm a full human soul in Christ. Athanasius insisted that Christ was real flesh, which truly suffered. But in his descriptions of the humanity of Christ the question of a human soul is not explicitly treated. Thus Christ is Logos plus flesh, not Logos plus flesh plus human soul.

Apollinaris of Laodicea was the first to present a formal definition of the content of the humanity of Christ.[44] He was a friend of Athanasius and a fellow defender of Nicaea. What may have been implicit in Athanasius is explicit in Apollinaris—he

---

also was founded upon a soteriology of imitation: Robert Gregg and Dennis Groh, *Early Arianism—A View of Salvation* (Philadelphia: Fortress, 1981).

[44] Sources for Apollinaris' writings, which consist entirely of the fragments that remain after his condemnation as a heretic, are to be found in H. Lietzmann, *Apollinaris von Laodicea und seine Schule* (Tübingen: J. C. B. Mohr, 1904). See also C. E. Raven, *Apollinarianism* (Cambridge and New York, 1923); Ekkehard Mühlenberg, *Apollinaris von Laodicea* (Göttingen: Vandenhoeck & Ruprecht, 1969); C. Kannengiesser, "Une nouvelle interprétation de la christologie d'Apollinaire," *Revue des sciences religieuses* 59 (1971): 27-36; and H. de Riedmatten, "Some Neglected Aspects of Apollinarist Christology," *Dominican Studies* 1 (1948): 139-60.

categorically denies that Christ had a human soul. What the Logos replaced in Christ was not the lower, animal soul, but the rational soul, and that because the fallen condition of the race consists in the corruption of its higher spiritual principle. In the joining of the perfect principle of intelligence and spirit, the Logos, with a human body, is the restoration of incorruptibility and impassibility to all humanity. What lies behind Apollinaris' theory is the philosophical principle that the human soul is a derivative of the divine nature. Thus, Apollinaris saw the uniting of the Logos with flesh as the reconstitution of humanity in perfection.

Although his theory was eventually rejected, at least two of Apollinaris' emphases are carried over by Alexandrian writers and introduced at the Council of Chalcedon. The *communicatio idiomatum*, or exchange of properties, was already a popular understanding and as such is reflected in liturgy before the fourth century, but Apollinaris drew the principle out to its extremes. The flesh of Christ could be called divine and the Logos could be called human because of the perfect union between them. Secondly, that union resulted in "one incarnate nature of the divine Logos." Ironically, Cyril of Alexandria used the phrase enthusiastically thinking it had originated with Athanasius.

A quite different emphasis was developing in Antioch among men like Diodore of Tarsus and his pupil Theodore of Mopsuestia who represent the same school of thinking as Nestorius under whom the christological controversy broke out in full force in the early fifth century. Diodore is best known for his commitment to an historical/grammatical hermeneutic, and, secondarily as one who emphasized the full humanity of Christ to the extent that a significant distinction remains between the Logos and the humanity even after the union—if there is in fact a union.[45] The

---

[45] Alois Grillmeier has questioned whether or not Diodore's Christology is typically "Antiochene" insofar as Diodore uses "flesh" to describe the humanity of Christ. *Christ in Christian Tradition*, vol. 1, rev. ed., trans. J. Bowden (Atlanta: John Knox, 1975), pp. 355 ff. Rowan Greer has responded by showing that Diodore does reflect the basic exegetical and philosophical presuppositions of

trend is even more evident in his pupil, Thedore of Mopsuestia, Chrysostom's close contemporary.[46]

Theodore is often used as the classic example of the Word-man Christology, the hallmark of which is the affirmation of a complete human nature, including a rational soul, in Christ. An explicit rejection of Apollinarism, this view avoids making the Logos the subject of the passible human characteristics and functions of the incarnate Christ. Because there are two natures that are each a distinct hypostasis, the sufferings of Christ do not involve the divine nature in any sort of mutability.

But there is an important set of anthropological and soteriological considerations behind the "assumed man" theory. Unlike Apollinaris and Athanasius who saw an essential link between the being of man and the being of God, Theodore and others envisioned a clearcut distinction of being which meant that in salvation the human element of moral transformation is more the point than a mystical reconstitution of being. Thus the incarnation is seen as that unique event in which a real human life, the "man of the Lord," accomplished the moral end that had been the purpose of human life in the first place. What distinguishes such a view from adoptionism is the acceptance of the principle of unity between the natures which obtained from the very start of the incarnation. It is a real unity, Theodore maintained, but one in which two hypostases, not one, come together.

In the next generation after Chrysostom the clash of the two Christologies occurred between Nestorius (second successor to Chrysostom as bishop of Constantinople) and Cyril of

---

other teachers of Antioch. R. A. Greer, "The Antiochene Christology of Diodore of Tarsus," *J Th St* N.S. 17 (1966): 327-41.

[46] For Theodore's Christology see: R. A. Greer, *Theodore of Mopsuestia: Exegete and Theologian* (London, 1961); R. A. Norris, *Manhood and Christ: A Study in the Christology of Theodore of Mopsuestia* (Oxford, 1963); F. A. Sullivan, *The Christology of Theodore of Mopsuestia* (Rome, 1956); J. L. McKenzie, "Annotations on the Christology of Theodore of Mopsuestia," *Th St* 19 (1958): 345-73; and Joanne Dewart, "The Notion of 'Person' Underlying the Christology of Theodore of Mopsuestia," *Stud Patr* 12 (1975): 199-207.

Alexandria. The terminology developed further, and culminated in the Chalcedonian definition. What Chrysostom provides is a look into the developing strains of thought in Christologies in large part determined by their corresponding soteriologies.

## Studies of Chrysostom's Christology

The few studies that have been done of Chrysostom's Christology in the past include a German dissertation by Juzek in 1912,[47] a more recent dissertation by Barnard[48] which treated both Christology and soteriology, and several articles, the most important of which was done by Camillus Hay[49] on Chrysostom's view of the human nature of Christ.

Juzek maintains that Chrysostom reflects essentially the Chalcedonian understanding of the unity of Christ and the relationship between the two natures. He shows first of all how Chrysostom's uses the same grammatical/historical hermeneutic as do his fellow Antiochenes. Also, christologically, Chrysostom is like them in the assertion of two complete natures: "Die Betonung der Integrität der zwei Naturen in Christus bildet auch bei Chrysostomus, wie bei seinen Landsleuten, einen eisernen Bestandteil seiner Christologie."[50] Although Chrysostom's use of temple and indwelling imagery indicates a theory of two distinguishable and complete natures in Christ, Juzek maintains that he does not use the terminology to keep the natures distinct after the union as do Theodore of Mopsuestia and Diodore.[51]

---

[47] J. H. Juzek, *Die Christologie des hl. Johannes Chrysostomus: Zugleich ein Beitrag zur Dogmatik der Antiochener* (Breslau, 1912).

[48] L. R. Barnard, "Christology and Soteriology in the Preaching of John Chrysostom" (dissertation, Southwestern Baptist Theological Seminary, 1974).

[49] Camillus Hay, "St. John Chrysostom and the Integrity of the Human Nature of Christ," *Franciscan Studies* 19 (1959): 298-317.

[50] Juzek, *Die Christologie*, p. 31.

[51] "Chrysostomus redet wie Theodor davon, daß in Christus der Logos wie in einem Hause und Tempel gewohnt habe—ein Bild, das er zu wiederholten Malen anwendet—so ist das insofern unrichtig und der Meinung des Heiligen entgegen, als Chrysostomus wohl die Integrität der beiden Naturen bewahrt, aber nicht in

But neither can it be said of Chrysostom that he can be identified with the Alexandrian cause. He maintains much more of a distinction between the natures than would Cyril, for instance, in his assertion of two wills in Christ and two centers of activity. Juzek concludes that while Chrysostom did not and could not have reflected the terminology of Chalcedon like "hypostatic union," he nevertheless demonstrated essentially the same understanding, avoiding both the dangers of denying a real union or denying a real human nature.[52]

Hay writes particularly to dispute the view of Juzek that Chrysostom emphasized the integrity of the human nature of Christ. The main difference of opinion involves the interpretation of σάρξ, that is, whether it means in Chrysostom's use simply the flesh or body of Christ, or whether it designates a complete human nature including rational soul. Hay sees no reason to see it as more than flesh. Where Chrysostom elaborates on the fears or anguish of Christ, as in the scene in the garden of Gethsemane, he is not indicating more than that the flesh has natural defenses which react to imminent danger. This too is the explanation for Chrysostom's description of two wills opposed to each other when Christ prayed "not my will but thine be done." Even though Chrysostom makes explicit references to a soul in Christ, Hay maintains that nothing more is meant than the lower, animal soul. There is no evidence of Chrysostom's describing distinct operations of the human nature of Christ and there certainly is no reference to an independent intellectual capability. When he does need to make a direct response to the Apollinarist heresy,

---

der Weise des Thedor, als ob er die menschliche Natur in Christus verselbständige und als ob der Logos nur κατ᾽ εὐδοκίαν in Christus wohne, sondern er läßt eine ἕνωσις der beiden Naturen stattfinden. Der Logos wohnt nicht als ἐνέργεια, sondern als eigene selbständige οὐσία in der menschlichen Natur" (Juzek, *Die Christologie*, p. 16).

[52] While Juzek has many helpful things to say on some of the most important texts, one difficulty is the use of at least one text (quoted three times) that is now considered spurious. So, Baur points out that the use of the doubtful *hom. in Christi Nat.* (PG 56, 387) is clearly unwise. Baur, *John Chrysostom*, vol. 1, p. 367.

Chrysostom does affirm a human soul, and thus the integrity of the human nature of Christ; but such statements are rare, and it would thus seem best to conclude that a full humanity has no theological significance for Chrysostom.

In his detailed survey of Christologies of the first five centuries Alois Grillmeier agrees with Hay's estimation: "The typically Antiochene difficulties in the interpretation of the unity in Christ do not exist for Chrysostom. . . . This Antiochene, so persecuted by the Alexandrians, is far more Alexandrian than Antiochene in his Christology—a new indication of the care with which we must use a word like 'school.' Only with Theodore of Mopsuestia. . . does 'Antiochene' Christology properly begin."[53]

Barnard's study, on the other hand, defends the traditional view that Chrysostom reflects the anthropological, soteriological, and christological assumptions of the Antiochene school: "It is likely that Chrysostom escaped obloquy and oblivion because he differed from Antiochene theology only in respect to the doctrine of *apokatastasis*, for there is little difference between his Christology and the condemned christologies of Theodore and Nestorius."[54]

In the light of such divergences of interpretation, a fresh and detailed examination of Chrysostom's Christology is warranted.

---

[53] Grillmeier, *Christ in Christian Tradition*, p.421.

[54] Barnard, "Christology and Soteriology," p. 67.

*Chapter Two*

# Chrysostom on
# the Divinity of Christ

## *Jesus and the Gospels*

In this and the following two chapters we will be examining three fundamental christological issues in Chrysostom's teaching: the divinity of Christ, the humanity of Christ, and the relationship between the divinity and the humanity. Because many of the texts we will be treating come from the homilies on the gospels, we pause here to note the particular hermeneutical questions relating to Chrysostom's understanding of Jesus in the gospels.

Virtually all the ancient theologians used the Scriptures in the substance of their discussions, but they differ widely in the degree that their discussions center around the key christological passages of the New Testament. Because Chrysostom's theological method was systematic exposition of Scripture, his Christology is primarily found in his analysis of biblical texts and his response to the interpretations of others.[55]

---

[55] There have been many studies of Chrysostom's hermeneutics because his many sermons and commentaries provide an unusually rich source for studying the more historical exegesis of the Antiochenes. F. H. Chase, *A Study of the History of Biblical Interpretation* (Cambridge, 1887); S. Haidacher, *Die Lehre des heiligen Johannes Chrysostomus über die Schriftinspiration* (Salzburg, 1897); M. H. Flanagan, *St. John Chrysostom's Doctrine of Condescension and Accuracy in the Scriptures* (Napier, 1948); B. H. Vandenberghe, *Saint Jean Chrysostome et la Parole de Dieu* (Paris, 1961); R. Hill, "St. John Chrysostom's Teaching on Inspiration in 'Six Homilies on Isaiah,'" *Vig Chr* 22 (1968): 19-37.

Perhaps the priority Chrysostom placed on doctrines relating to the person and work of Christ determined that the majority of his preaching would concentrate on the New Testament books. And of the homilies on the New Testament, the series on Matthew and on John are longer than those on other books.[56] The gospels hold a special fascination for Chrysostom.[57] They supply the raw material for his Christology especially on humanity of Christ, and thus it will be helpful before coming to the texts involved to understand Chrysostom's general approach to the testimonies of the Evangelists.

Before embarking upon a long season of preaching from one of the gospels Chrysostom prepared his congregation with an introductory address on the biblical book at hand. Here he reveals some of his own presuppositions about the gospels and their authors. His objective was to instill in his listeners a sense of privilege in being able to hear the holy words of the apostles. To open the book of Matthew is "to set foot within the holy vestibule"[58] and to listen to the inspired words of John is denied those who are dull, sleepy, or "unwilling to be freed from this swinish life."[59] Consideration of the message of the Evangelists is not speculation about metaphysical abstractions, but the exposing of one's life to the authority of God by reflecting on the Savior himself.

That Chrysostom's view of Christ is derived from a historical approach to the gospels is especially evident in the homilies on Matthew. Because of his approach Chrysostom sometimes gets bogged down in details of fact and considers only briefly the mysterious aspects of the gospels. At times he almost apologizes when a sermon's time has run out and a problem of fact or

---

[56] Of the more than 600 sermons of Chrysostom extant, 178 are on the Gospels of Matthew and John.

[57] See T. R. McKibbens, "The Exegesis of John Chrysostom: Homilies on the Gospels," *Expository Times* 93 (June 1982): 264-70.

[58] *Hom. in Matt.* 2, 1 (PG 57, 23).

[59] *Hom. in Jn.* 1, 2 (PG 59, 27).

controversy has gotten more attention than some of the profound truths of a passage. Nevertheless, this more scientific approach means that Chrysostom's conclusions line up more closely with the intent of the gospel writers than a more allegorical approach would.[60]

In his introductory homilies on Matthew Chrysostom calls the gospel "history,"[61] and almost immediately addresses the question of discrepancies among the gospels. There are, he says, those sects that have solved the difficulties by simply excising some of the record.[62] Instead, the gospels can be seen as four different accounts of the incarnation which, even if they appear to contradict each other on some points, all assert the cardinal points of the Christian message.

> But what are these points? Such as follows: that God became man, that he wrought miracles, that he was crucified, that he was buried, that he rose again, that he ascended, that he will judge, that he has given commandments tending to salvation, that he has brought in a law not contrary to the Old Testament, that he is a Son, that he is only-begotten, that he is a true Son, that he is of the same substance [τῆς αὐτῆς οὐσίας] with the Father, and as many things as are like these.[63]

The gospels, then, are accounts of the Son both as a historical figure and as the object of faith described in the creeds, most especially, the creed of Nicaea. The gospel accounts do not need to be looked at allegorically in order to discover their highest teachings about Christ. Matthew and John are straightforward discourses about heavenly things given through a real publican and a real fisherman. These authors have provided a φιλοσοφία,

---

[60] J. D. Quinn, "Saint John Chrysostom on History in the Synoptics," *Catholic Biblical Quarterly* 24 (April 1962): 140-7 refers to Chrysostom's "extraordinary sensitivity to the human literary form employed by the evangelists" (p. 142).

[61] Ἱστορία in *Hom. in Matt.* 1, 2 and 1, 3 (PG 57, 16 and 17).

[62] That way, chosen by Marcion, met with determined opposition in the early third century from Tertullian and others up to Chrysostom's own time.

[63] *Hom. in Matt.* 1, 2 (PG 57, 16).

compared to which Plato's Republic is "ridiculous," and "indistinct," consisting of "lines without number."[64] One cannot help but hear in such comparisons the preference Chrysostom had for a philosophy based on historical revelation rather than on metaphysical speculation.

But what about discrepancies between the accounts? Whereas Origen identifies different spiritual meanings coming from contradictory passages, Chrysostom tries to find the συμφωνία; in fact, he promises the congregation he will establish the συμφωνία.[65] His concern for details of fact, however, is less than that for the important doctrinal points listed above. Where discrepancies are apparent, they involve only matters of time (καιρός), place (τόπος), or the words themselves (ῥημάτων αὐτῶν).[66] Chrysostom only occasionally discusses such points and then tries vigorously to harmonize the accounts.[67] His basic assumption is that the gospel writers differ in style, but not content. The same principle applies to internal difficulties within a particular book. For instance, Chrysostom assumes that the presence of two temple cleansing accounts in John means that Jesus performed the act twice.[68] The reference in Mk. 2:26 to Abiathar the high priest (instead of Ahimelech) means the man had two names.[69]

Chrysostom encounters a historical problem in the Gospel of Matthew almost immediately—the genealogy of Christ. Though problematic and seemingly boring, taken by some as "superfluous" and "a mere numbering of names,"[70] this genealogy,

---

[64] *Hom. in Matt.* 1, 5 (PG 57, 19).

[65] *Hom. in Matt.* 1, 3 (PG 57, 17).

[66] *Hom. in Matt.* 1, 2 (PG 57, 16). Such minor discrepancies in fact prove the reliability of the accounts, says Chrysostom, because identical wording would be evidence of collusion among the Evangelists.

[67] Quinn counts only eleven such discussions in the first forty-four homilies on Matthew, and all but three are handily harmonized.

[68] *Hom. in Jn.* 23, 2 (PG 59, 139).

[69] *Hom. in Matt.* 39, 1 (PG 57, 435).

[70] *Hom. in Matt.* 1, 6 (PG 57, 21).

says Chrysostom, is an important text. It is, after all, the beginning of "the book of the generation of Jesus Christ," and nothing is more important than his generation.[71] Persistent questions are raised by the passage. Why is Joseph's genealogy included, since Jesus' only real link with humanity was through Mary? Chrysostom's less-than-satisfactory answer is that the Virgin Birth, because of its potential for scandal, was disguised. Mary was of David's line, but for expediency only Joseph's line is delineated. Why does the genealogy include such questionable characters as Tamar and Rahab? There is a theological explanation here. Not only did Christ lower himself by taking flesh and becoming man, but by having such a lineage, he showed that he was "in no respect ashamed of our evils."[72] Why does Mark exclude a genealogy and Luke have a longer one? Matthew set the standard while Mark shortened the version and Luke drew it out, comparable to their respective mentors, Peter and Paul, who displayed the same tendencies.

Such questions—still asked by modern commentators, not necessarily with the same answers—show Chrysostom's overall approach to the book. When matters of fact and history present themselves, they are to be interpreted as such. Chrysostom does say that the genealogical names themselves afford great opportunity for finding a θεωρία or spiritual sense,[73] the word preferred by the Antiochenes for a scriptural meaning that is somewhere between the literal and the fancifully allegorical.[74] But the examples of names and their meanings that he gives— Abraham, Jacob, Solomon, Zerubbabel—are names that have demonstrable Hebrew etymologies, a fact that once again shows

---

[71] Matthew's use of "generation" was in a purely historical sense.

[72] *Hom. in Matt.* 3, 2 (PG 57, 34).

[73] *Hom. in Matt.* 4, 2 (PG 57, 41).

[74] Cf. Lampe, *A Patristic Greek Lexicon*, s.v. θεωρία. However, θεωρία can also be used in the same sense as ἀλληγορία by the Cappadocians and those associated with Alexandria such as Philo and Origen.

the lack of desire in Chrysostom to seek an allegorical sense for a passage.[75]

The first homily on the Gospel of John differs from that on Matthew in the degree of spiritual significance Chrysostom assigns to it.[76] His introduction to "the spiritual Gospel," as Maurice Wiles has called it,[77] is as lyrical as Chrysostom gets. The voice of the son of thunder, a well-fashioned and jewelled lyre, is contrasted with the noise of rhetoricians, musicians, and athletes who daily demand the attention of Chrysostom's Antiochene congregation. John is a messenger sent from heaven, who is not of this world, and "has speaking within him the Comforter, the Omnipresent." Yet alongside these rhetorical flourishes Chrysostom shows his historical interest in the book, beginning with its author and his humble origins as a fisherman from Bethsaida. In eighty-eight homilies he comments on dozens of events in the historical life and ministry of Jesus, almost always assuming that each journey or confrontation or miracle has a message behind it.[78]

---

[75] Robert Grant describes the basic hermeneutical differences between the Alexandrians and the Antiochenes: "The school of Antioch insisted on the historical reality of the biblical revelation. They were unwilling to lose it in a world of symbols and shadows. . . . Where the Alexandrines use the word 'theory' as equivalent to allegorical interpretation, the Antiochene exegetes use it for a sense of scripture higher or deeper than the literal or historical meaning, but firmly based on the letter. This understanding does not deny the literal meaning of scripture but is grounded on it, as an image is based on the thing represented and points toward it. Both image and thing are comprehensible at the same time" (*The Bible in the Church: A Short History of Interpretation* [New York: Macmillan, 1948], pp. 76f.).

[76] John "does not begin like the rest from beneath, but from above." He is "more lofty than the rest" (*Hom. in Matt.* 1, 3 [PG 57, 17]).

[77] Maurice Wiles, *The Spiritual Gospel* (Cambridge, 1959). Wiles provides an excellent analysis of how the fourth Gospel was used in the developing theology of the patristic period.

[78] Allegorizing a text is not only convenient for the apologist, but also for the homilist, who may hold his audience's attention by drawing out of an otherwise ordinary passage a mysterious spiritual meaning. Yet Chrysostom remains committed to avoiding reading such meanings into the accounts of the life and

The fourth Gospel is in many ways the gospel that supplies fuel for the trinitarian speculations of the second and third centuries, the Arian controversy of the fourth, and the christological debates of the fourth and fifth centuries and beyond. T. E. Pollard puts it this way:

> It was St. John's gospel, with the Logos-concept of the Prologue, which opened the way for the misinterpretations of the Christian message as a Word-theology and as a Logos-theology. It was, however, the same gospel that also provided the basis for the refutation of both these misinterpretations and for the establishment of a theology in which Jesus Christ is central as the Son of God who became man for us men and our salvation.[79]

John's Gospel thus receives considerable attention from Chrysostom because he sees in it both the sources for the questions about the incarnate Christ and the corresponding answers. It is a book for refuting gnostic denials of the reality of the bodily incarnation, Jewish and Arian rejection of the deity of Christ, and Sabellian and Marcellian ignorance of the distinct hypostasis of the Son. Here Chrysostom has to deal with some of the most explicit passages about the emotions of Jesus, his deference to the Father, and claims to deity. His explanations often betray a kind of second-guessing of the actions and words of Christ, but always, they represent a grappling with passages he assumes to be historically grounded.

## The Neo-Arian Movement

Just before one of the most significant councils of the early church was convened in Constantinople in 381 to address the

---

ministry of Jesus, as, for example, when he explains that the soldier's inability to divide Christ's garment does not mean (as many evidently had said) that it was woven from the top, indicating that Christ received his divinity from above. If anything, the statement shows that Christ wore ordinary and plain clothing. *Hom. in Jn.* 85, 1-2 (PG 59, 461).

[79] T. E. Pollard, *Johannine Christology and the Early Church* (Cambridge, 1970), p. 319.

ongoing problem of Arianism (and the new theological aberration of Apollinaris), John Chrysostom had been ordained to the diaconate by bishop Melitius of Antioch. The radical Arians, labelled in modern times as Neo-Arians but in their own time as Anomoeans because they supposedly claimed that the Son is unlike (ἀνόμοιος) the Father in essence, had already lost most of their prominence and power in ecclesiastical circles. The last significant Neo-Arian treatise had been written by its last major leader, Eunomius; and just a few years after the council Eunomius would be banished by emperor Theodosius and Neo-Arian meetings restricted both in the cities and in the countryside.

Nevertheless, five years later, soon after Chrysostom was ordained to the priesthood, he preached dozens of sermons against the Neo-Arians. The movement was dying, but not dead. It is primarily the polemic against the Neo-Arians that is the occasion for Chrysostom's teaching on the nature of God and on the divine nature of Christ. In particular, his earlier sermons preached in Antioch—those on the Gospel of John and the series *On the Incomprehensible Nature of God*—have the greatest concentration of statements explaining the deity of Christ. After surveying the Neo-Arian movement itself, we will examine first the philosophical objections Chrysostom presents, then the exegetical arguments.

### Philosophical and Historical Roots

Two recent studies of Arianism[80] show the important distinction between the early and later Arians. Robert Gregg's and Dennis Groh's study of Arius and his contemporaries, *Early*

---

[80] Among numerous other new studies. Note Joseph T. Lienhard, "Recent Studies in Arianism," *Religious Studies Review* 8 (1982): 330-37; Charles Kannengiesser, "Arius and the Arians," *Th St* 44 (1983): 456-75; ibid., "The Athanasian Decade 1974-84: A Bibliographical Report," *Th St* 46 (1985): 524-41; and the collection of some twenty-two papers on Arianism all given at the Ninth International Conference on Patristic Studies at Oxford in 1983: Robert C. Gregg, ed., *Arianism: Historical and Theological Reassessments* (Cambridge, Mass.: The Philadelphia Patristic Foundation, 1985).

*Arianism—A View of Salvation* presents a revision of the traditional interpretation of Arius. Arius' insistence on the creaturely status of the Son, say Gregg and Groh, has a soteriological rather than a cosmological basis.[81]

The early Arianism of the 320's may be contrasted with its later stages of the late 350's through the early 380's. Thomas Kopecek's very detailed study of this period, *A History of Neo-Arianism*[82] begins with a brief recounting of early Arianism, then proceeds to an examination of the teachings of the two great Neo-Arian proponents Aëtius and Eunomius and their polemical dealings with Athanasius and the Cappadocians, and concludes with the tensions between John Chrysostom and the Neo-Arians of Antioch and Constantinople. What follows summarizes what Kopecek has observed in the primary sources of this later period.

What is fundamental to Arianism in both its earlier and later stages (and evidenced at least as early as Justin) is the understanding that a primary characteristic of God is ungeneratedness, and conversely, that a primary characteristic of the Son is generatedness. This is where Arius began; and because moderates like Eusebius of Caeserea had the same understanding, the Council of Nicaea—although it condemned Arius' teaching— was far from a permanent settlement of the trinitarian question. To the Arians it was ungeneratedness that distinguished God from the rest of creation. Another key factor in the development of Arian theology was the fact that two closely related and nearly identical words, "ungenerated" (ἀγένητος) and "unbegotten"

---

[81] "The central point in the Arian system is that Christ gains and holds his sonship in the same way as other creatures. Arius' doctrine that Christ was advanced to God by adoption contains the ground and definition of the faith and hope of believers. The early Arians portrayed Christ as they did because the advocacy of this Christology gave fullest expression to their understanding of the content and dynamic of salvation." Gregg and Groh, *Early Arianism*, p. 50.

[82] Two vols. (Cambridge, Mass.: The Philadelphia Patristic Foundation, 1979).

(ἀγέννητος), were being used interchangeably.[83] Thus, the bibical attribution of the begottenness of the Son, was, to the Arians, no different than that of generatedness, and so the Son could not be compared to God the Father in essence in any way.

Two assumptions, then, lay behind the basic conviction of the Arians that the Son cannot be considered homoousion with the Father. First, that the Son's begottenness meant that he was generated; and second, that the one and only true God is chiefly characterized by his essential ungeneratedness. One of the most significant differences between Arius himself and later Arians is that, while Arius thought the essence of God was unknowable, later Arians came to insist that God's essence is indeed knowable, and that that essence is ungeneratedness itself.[84] The Neo-Arians like Aëtius and Eunomius, in other words, move to the center of the debate the characteristic that they thought made the essential unlikeness of the Father and the Son a certainty. As we will see later when we examine the texts, Chrysostom makes his most fundamental attack on the Neo-Arians on precisely this point— the unknowability of the essence of God.[85]

---

[83] *Agenetos* from γίνομαι, to become; and *agennetos* from γεννάω, to beget. G. L. Prestige explains: "As soon as theology turned from theism to Christology, the spelling *agennetos* raised the most agonizing difficulties, and in fact provided one of the main pivots for the Arian heresy. Christ was not *agennetos*: He was the Son of the Father; was He therefore to be reckoned among *geneta*?... It would seem that there is nothing much to choose between *agennetos* and *agenetos*, except a vague sense of the greater propriety of the personal term in connection with the personal being. We are dealing with alternative spellings of a single word, in fact, rather than with two separate terms bearing distinct connotations" (*God in Patristic Thought* [London: SPCK, 1952], p. 43). Kopecek notes that Athanasius distinguishes what previous authors (and he himself) had equated, ἀγέννητος and ἀγένητος: "Correlative to God as ἀγέννητος is the begotten Son, τὸ γέννημα; correlative to God as ἀγένητος are all generated things, τὰ γενητά. This threefold ontology of God ὁ ἀγέννητος/ἀγένητος, his Son τὸ γέννημα, and his creations τὰ γενητά would later come into its own with the Cappadocian Fathers" (p. 91).

[84] As early as Asterius, one of the early Arians (d. after 341), there is a departure from Arius' conviction of the unknowability of God's essence.

[85] Thus, the title of one important series of sermons: Περὶ ἀκαταλήπτου, "On the Incomprehensible Nature of God."

The Neo-Arian period, beginning some twenty-five years after Arius, was dominated by the figures of Aëtius and his disciple Eunomius. Aëtius died in 367, almost a decade before Chrysostom preached against the Neo-Arians, but Eunomius was still living well into Chrysostom's career. Aëtius forged his ideas in the heat of debate with those who would rally around either *homoousion* or *homoiousion* as the definitive statement of the relationship of the Son with the Father. The Homoousians, led by Athanasius and a few others, struggled in an uphill battle with most eastern opinions, which seemed either inclined to declare the Son of a different substance than the Father (ἀνόμοιος or ἑτεροούσιος) or, at the most, of like substance with the Father (ὁμοιούσιος). The latter position was first clearly delineated in the *Ekthesis Makrostichos* (Creed of the Long Lines) of 344, thought by its authors to be a solution to the excesses of Arius on the one side and of Marcellus and, to some degree, Athanasius on the other side. Instead, homoeousianism served to further motivate both the radical Arian Aëtius and Athanasius to continue to pursue their opposite theologies.

From 346 to 356 Aëtius was a teacher at various times in both Antioch and Alexandria. He was able successfully to promote his ideas among students who would become influential bishops in Asia Minor and directly oppose Athanasius.[86] Although the Council of Ancyra[87] in 358 rejected the formula "unlike-in-essence," Aëtius maintained his position and gave it even fuller definition in his *Syntagmation* of 359, a collection of syllogisms that were designed to demonstrate that because of the essential ungeneratedness of God and the generatedness of the Son, the two cannot be conceived but as unlike-in-essence.[88] Thus, by 360 Arianism had moved into a new and fuller self-definition. The

---

[86] Kopecek, *Neo-Arianism*, p. 114.

[87] See Joseph T. Lienhard, "The Epistle of the Synod of Ancyra, 358: A Reconsideration" in Gregg, *Arianism*, pp. 313-19.

[88] Aëtius avoided using the controversial terms ἀνόμοιος and ἑτεροούσιος.

detailed and complex syllogisms of the *Syntagmation* were a formidable challenge for both Homoousians and Homoeousians.

The classic form of Neo-Arianism was established. Kopecek summarizes the position in three points. The first two are early Arian claims: there is only one being who is ungenerated; and God is comprehensible to the human mind (although Arius himself denied this). The third point comes from the Middle Platonic view "that names used in normal parlance are, in general, revelatory of the essences of the things named." The conclusion, therefore, must be that

> if God is comprehensible to men and ungeneratedness is the one characteristic differentiating him from all other things, ungeneratedness must be his name. And since names are revelatory of essences, God's essence must be ungenerated. The Son's essential generatedness, of course, is simply a logical deduction. ... Thus, if God is not only ungenerated but essentially so, and the Son not only generated, but essentially so, unlikeness in essence naturally follows.[89]

### Eunomius and Later Neo-Arianism

The height of the influence of the Neo-Arians occurred from 357 to 359 when both Antioch and Alexandria were under the leadership of Neo-Arian bishops. But the Anomoean ecclesiastical party continued to run into further theological opposition, for example at the Council of Ancyra of 358, which tried "to steer a middle course between the extremes of Neo-Arianism and Marcellan Sabellianism, but without limiting itself to vague scriptural language."[90]

A new and very significant element in the debate had arisen— the question of theological language. This epistemological concern would be raised many more times in the next twenty years of discussion. In particular, the Homoousians like Athanasius, and

---

[89] Kopecek, *Neo-Arianism*, p. 122.

[90] Kopecek, *Neo-Arianism*, p. 156.

the Homoeousians, maintained that the names Father and Son were most appropriate in theological definitions because of their scriptural precedent. Whereas ungenerated-generated language could only show the difference between God and the Son, Father-Son language allowed both distinction and unity. The *homoousion* and *homoiousion* formulas were much easier to defend when the titles of Father and Son were applied rather than the seemingly contradictory ungenerated-generated distinction.

The Neo-Arians avoided Father-Son language when speaking of God in essentialist terms. God may be spoken of as Father only in reference to his will, not his essence.[91] Otherwise, God would be seen to be changeable, and like all human fathers, subject to passion. The Neo-Arians would agree to likeness only between Father and Son interpreted in these terms. The radical unlikeness still pertains to the essential identities of the ungenerated God and his generated Logos. The likeness the Homoeousians spoke of went far beyond the likeness the Neo-Arians were willing to admit. Accordingly, they used Father and Son as terms that had reference to the essential identity of God.[92]

It comes as no surprise that, in connection with the debate over theological language, the Neo-Arians were often accused of using logic to an exaggerated extent and of ignoring scriptural revelation. Indeed, Aëtius's *Syntagmation* is composed entirely of syllogisms. Only one identifiable scriptural quotation can be found—its benediction. It is only in the later stages of Neo-Arianism, in the writings of Eunomius, that a beginning is made of

---

[91] So God is Father with reference to Christ in no different way from how he is Father to all human beings. Such, said the Neo-Arians, is suggested in Isa. 1:2; Mal. 2:10; Jn. 1:12-13; Job 38:28, and elsewhere. The Homoeousians responded with Eph. 3:14—"from whom every fatherhood in heaven and earth is named"— saying that earthly fatherhood is an analogy of, and is derived from, divine fatherhood. It is thus perfectly appropriate to refer to God as Father.

[92] Furthermore, the Homoeousians said that the ungenerated-generated categories of the Neo-Arians were only descriptive of the difference, whereas the Father-Son description of essence showed both difference and connection.

a distinctive Neo-Arian exegesis. Chrysostom often challenges this logic-chopping methodology of the Neo-Arians.

Neo-Arianism gradually lost its status as an ecclesiastical party and was excluded from the new alliances which were forming from late 359. A new party, the Homoeans, were content to set the language of *ousia* and *hypostasis* aside in favor of a simpler confession of the "likeness" of the Son to the Father. Athanasius had already shown some sympathy to the language of "likeness" as used by the Homoeousians saying that what they meant by *homoiousion* he meant by *homoousion*. The relative closeness of the *homoousian*, *homoeousian*, and *homoean* positions meant that the Neo-Arian theology became increasingly isolated.

Eunomius, the later leader of the Neo-Arian movement, agreed that there was no substantial difference between the "same-in-essence" and the "like-in-essence" positions. In direct contrast he continued the basic Arian insistence on the unlikeness-in-essence of God and Christ in his *Apologia* of c. 360. God's essence is completely comprehensible, said Eunomius, and that essence is ἀγεννησία, ungeneratedness. Eunomius' writings provided the occasion for new extensions of Nicene theology, provided by the Cappadocians Basil of Caesarea and Gregory of Nyssa. Basil's *Contra Eunomium* was a rebuttal of Eunomius' chief work, the *Apologia*; and Eunomius' reply to Basil eighteen years later, *Apologia Apologiae*, was in turn answered by Gregory in his *Contra Eunomium* (c. 382). Over a period of two decades the neo-Nicene theology of the Cappadocians was sharpened and refined by the ongoing polemic with the complex logical arguments of Eunomius.[93]

Basil, like Chrysostom after him, attacked Neo-Arianism on its claim that the essence of God is knowable. Many qualities or

---

[93] From 361 the Neo-Arians operated as an independent sect. Both Aëtius and Eunomius withdrew in 365. "Neither ever again ruled over an individual congregation, preferring—as had been their deepest tendency all along—a more detached, intellectual direction of the Neo-Arian movement" (Kopecek, *Neo-Arianism*, p. 424).

properties of God are knowable, including his ungeneratedness, but none of these is the essence of God. Since the essence of God lies beyond human comprehension (ἐπίνοια), there is no reason why a common essence between the Father and the Son cannot be maintained.[94] Whether the differences between the early Arians and the Homoousians were fundamentally cosmological or soteriological, those between the Neo-Arians and the Neo-Nicenes clearly ended up in the realm of epistemology.

## John Chrysostom and the Neo-Arians

The final decline of Neo-Arianism, during which Chrysostom was preaching in Antioch and Constantinople, occurred not only in the theological, but also in the political and ecclesiastical arenas. Starting in 380 emperor Theodosius maintained a policy that was unambiguously pro-Nicene. Gregory of Nazianzus was made bishop of Constantinople in 381, and later in 381 anti-Arian legislation was issued that increasingly restricted the meetings of Arian congregations. Neo-Arians continued to meet in private homes or attended the orthodox churches. According to Kopecek, it was because Chrysostom "was the kind of educated and intellectual Christian that the Neo-Arians believed would be at home in their favorite activity—theological dispute" that they attended his church services, engaged in theological discussion with him, and tried to engage him in theological debate.[95]

Chrysostom's homilies contain frequent allusions to the relationship of the Neo-Arians to the orthodox churches and to the tactics Chrysostom himself employs in the confrontation.

---

[94] "Basil held that virtually all our knowledge comes to us through our reflection upon sensible reality, that is, through *epinoia*. And language also is a product of this secondary reflection upon primary sense data. For Eunomius, none of our knowledge comes through such secondary reflection: it is innately ours in the words God has implanted in our psyches. Basil maintained, however, that our knowledge not only of earthly reality but also of heavenly reality comes through *epinoia*" (Kopecek, *Neo-Arianism*, p. 465f.).

[95] Kopecek, *Neo-Arianism*, p. 530.

While always combative, he nonetheless considers restoration and healing as the proper, and realistic, goal.

> But I hesitated and held back when I saw that men who were sick with this disease were listening to my words and finding pleasure in what I said. Since I did not wish to frighten off my prey, for a time I restrained my tongue from engaging in these contests with them. I wished to have them in perfect check before I stripped myself to face them in combat. But when I heard, thanks be to God, that they were clamoring and challenging me to enter the arena, it was then that I felt confident in my courage, readied myself for action, and took up the weapons "to destroy their sophistries and every proud pretention which raises itself against the knowledge of God"[96] . . . . These weapons do not inflict wounds; rather they cure those who are sick. Therefore, let us not be provoked with these men, let us not use anger as an excuse, but let us talk with them gently and with kindness.[97]

There was evidently a lively and vigorous day-by-day debate between Chrysostom and his heretical listeners:

> I will put before you an objection which the sons of the heretics have advanced against me. What is this objection? Yesterday I was discussing the power of the only begotten and I showed that his power is equal to the power of the Father who begot him. And I spent many a word on this subject. Although they were stunned and confounded by the arguments I gave, they have now advanced against me a gospel text. . . .[98]

On several occasions Chrysostom, in one statement, both instructs his congregation on how to respond to the Anomoeans in a loving way, and ridicules their inferior opinions:

> These are my reasons for enouraging all of you to speak to the Anomoeans mildly and with moderation. Try with all your might to treat them as you would treat people who have suffered a mental illness and lost their wits. Surely this

---

[96] 2 Cor. 10:5.

[97] *De Incomprehensibili* 1, 334-52 (Malingrey, pp. 131 f.).

[98] *De Incomprehensibili* 8, 1 (PG 48, 769).

doctrine of theirs is the offspring of their madness and of a mind swollen with great conceit. Their festering wounds cannot bear a touch of the hand nor endure too rough a contact. So it is that wise physicians cleanse such ulcers with a soft sponge. Since these Anomoeans have a festering ulcer in their souls, let us take a soft sponge, wet it with pure and soothing water, and bathe the ulcer with all the words I have spoken to you.[99]

Although both Anomoeans and orthodox were listening to the same sermons, Chrysostom distinguished the polemics from instruction. At one point, he claimed that the "battle with the heretics has come to an end," and thus "now we must drive all upset and doubt from the minds of our brothers. . . . For waging war and teaching are not the same, nor is it as easy to correct one's own brother as it is to wound a foe."[100] Chrysostom was, in fact, encountering a pastoral crisis, because the Anomoeans continued to be persuasive enough to present a serious threat. He alludes to the intense interest in the ongoing debate on the part of the Antiochene Christians:

I know well that each of you feels the birth pains of your desire to hear what I shall say about the Arian Anomoeans no less than I feel the pangs of my desire to tell you. The reason for this is that our city has loved Christ from the beginning.[101]

---

[99] *De Incomprehensibili* 2, 490-99 (Malingrey, p. 182).

[100] *De Incomprehensibili* 8, 4 (PG 48, 772).

[101] *De Incomprehensibili* 1, 35-39 (Malingrey pp. 96f.). Chrysostom's tactics in dealing with the threat of Arianism are threefold: a) direct response to the opponents themselves; b) doctrinal instruction for the congregation; e.g.: "That is why we must all come together here in church and drive back the onslaught of our foes. Do you say that you cannot preach a long discourse, that you have no instruction to give? Merely be present here in the church, and you have done everything you have to do" (*De Incomprehensibili* 11, 3 [PG 48, 801]); and c) protection for the faithful but "weak" in encouraging them to simply avoid the trouble-makers; e.g.: "if a man is one of the weaker sort, he does both harm to himself and to the invalid by exposing himself to contact with the sick. . . . Let us avoid any association with them" (*De Incomprehensibili* 2, 521-32 [Malingrey, p. 184]).

Twelve years later, in only his second homily to the church of Constantinople, Chrysostom still speaks of the threat of heresy by which he could only mean the scattered groups of Anomoeans who remained after Theodosius' legislation against them.

> If the Church of Antioch is older in terms of time, this Church of Constantinople is more fervent in its faith. . . . On every side wolves surround you, but your flock is not destroyed. A surging sea, storms, and waves have constantly encircled this sacred ship, but those who sail on it are not engulfed by the waters. The fires of heresy threaten with their encircling flames on every side, but those who are in the midst of the furnace enjoy the blessing of a heavenly dew. In like fashion, it is an unexpected and wonderful thing to see how this church has been planted in this section of the city. To see it here is like seeing an olive tree in bloom, weighted down with fruit, yet standing in the middle of a furnace.[102]

From his early years as a young priest in Antioch, then, until his final position as archbishop in the most important see in the East, Chrysostom of necessity expounds a Neo-Nicene Christology which includes a view of the divinity of Christ like that of the Cappadocians. We turn now to the specific philosophical and exegetical elements of his teaching.

### Chrysostom's Response to Neo-Arian Theology

Most of Chrysostom's polemical writings against the Neo-Arians or Anomoeans occur in the earlier part of his preaching career. In the lengthy homilies on Gospel of John, which were probably preached in the early 380's in Antioch, Chrysostom frequently disputes the Anomoeans. The content of the gospel itself—its statements of the unity of Father and Son and their

---

[102] De Incomprehensibili 11, 1 (PG 48, 797). Even though by the time Chrysostom began preaching in Constantinople in early 398 Theodosius' decrees had been in effect for almost two decades, Neo-Arian theology evidently continued to be an issue at least in memory if not in open debate. That the "fires of heresy" should continue to at least smoulder is not surprising given the domination of the Arians in Constantinople for the better part of four decades (339-379).

distinctions, and of the cosmic Christ—naturally made it the substance of controversy. That may in fact be the reason Chrysostom chose to preach an extended series on John so early in his career.

Of more direct interest, however, is his series of homilies directly addressing the Anomoeans: Περὶ ἀκαταλήπτου, *On the Incomprehensible Nature of God.* The first five of these twelve homilies come from Chrysostom's first year of preaching in Antioch, and the next five were probably also delivered in Antioch soon thereafter. The last two were delivered in Chrysostom's early days as archbishop of Constantinople.[103] Of the homilies Emmanuel Amand de Mendieta says:

> Cette doctrine et en particulier cet adjectif ἀκατάληπτος revient à presque toutes les pages des cinq homélies de Jean Chrysostome sur l'incompréhensibilité de l'essence divine. D'ailleurs cette doctrine de l'extrême transcendance de l'essence même de Dieu constitue l'une des doctrines fondamentales de l a théologie de Jean, prêtre d'Antioche et archevêque de Constantinople. C'est l'une des notes les plus profondes et les plus émouvantes dans la symphonie des oeuvres de notre saint.[104]

We will proceed by distinguishing the philosophical and the exegetical arguments of Chrysostom against the Anomeans.

## Philosophical Considerations

While Chrysostom's defense of the deity of the Son consists in the main of exegetical arguments, he necessarily raises

---

[103] The first series of five have been critically edited by A.-M. Malingrey, SC, vol. 28, 2nd ed. (Paris: 1970), and all twelve homilies are translated by Paul W. Harkins FC, vol.72 (Washington, D. C., 1984). On the manuscript tradition of these homilies see A.-M. Malingrey, "La tradition manuscrite des homélies de Jean Chrysostome De Incomprehensibili," *Stud Patr* 10 (1970): 22-28.

[104] Emmanuel Amand De Mendieta, "L'incompréhensibilité de l'Essence divine d'après Jean Chrysostome," in *ΣΥΜΠΟΣΙΟΝ: Studies on St. John Chrysostom,* ed. Panayotis Christou (Thessaloniki: Patriarchal Institute for Patristic Studies, 1973), p. 23.

philosophical considerations if only because arguments of this sort were almost exclusively the mainstay of the Neo-Arian method. We will note Chrysostom's epistemology, then his view of the use of religious language in particular as it relates to the names of God, and finally, his evaluation of philosophical method itself.

The primary epistemological issue according to Chrysostom is indicated in the title of the series of sermons which are his most direct attack on Neo-Arianism: *On the Incomprehensible Nature of God*. Chrysostom's invective against the Anomoeans on this point is stronger than that directed against any other theological opponent:

> Let us try to tear out by the roots this destructive force because in it we have the mother of all evils, the source from which those teachings of the Anomoeans grew. What is the root of all these evils? Believe me, a holy trembling lays hold of me as I am about to speak of it. I tremble to let my tongue utter the thought they are constantly pondering in their minds. What, then, is the root of these evils? A mere human has the boldness to say: "I know God as God himself knows himself."[105]

There is one simple reason for affirming the incomprehensibility of God: it is the necessary consequence of his transcendence. Knowledge of God in his essence is not a capability of any member of the created order, but only of the Trinity itself as noted in a passage which contains a whole string of negations of human knowledge:

> Let us call upon him, then, as the ineffable (τὸν ἀνέκφραστον) God who is beyond our intelligence (τὸν ἀπερινόητον), invisible (τὸν ἀόρατον), incomprehensible (τὸν ἀκατάληπτον), who transcends the power of mortal words. Let us call on him as the God who is inscrutable (τὸν ἀνεξιχνίαστον) to the angels, unseen (τὸν ἀθέατον) by the Seraphim, inconceivable (τὸν ἀκατανόητον) to the Cherubim, invisible (τὸν ἀόρατον) to the principalities, to the powers, and to the virtues, in fact, to all

---

[105] *De Incomprehensibili* 2, 149-59 (Malingrey, p. 154).

creatures without qualification, because he is known only by the Son and the Spirit.[106]

The transcendence of God means the radical distinction between divine and human natures: "The distance between the essence of God and the essence of man is so great that no words can express it, nor is the mind capable of measuring it."[107]

It should not be difficult to admit the incomprehensibility of God if we do not comprehend even our own nature: "We do not even know well the essence of our own soul. . . . is it air, a breath, a wind, or fire?"[108] Nor, for that matter, do human beings fully comprehend other parts of the creation including angels and the firmament.[109]

This limited agnosticism falls somewhere between an abject ignorance of the nature of God and his ways, and the overly-confident assumption of essential knowledge. Human beings are left knowing the "that" (ὅτι) but not necessarily the "how" (πῶς).

> I, too, know many things but I do not know how to explain them. I know that God is everywhere and I know that he is everywhere in his whole being. But I do not know how he is everywhere. I know that he is eternal and has no beginning. But I do not know how. My reason (λογισμός) fails to grasp how it is possible for an essence (οὐσία) to exist when that essence has received its existence neither from itself nor from another. I know that he begot a son. But I do not know how. I know that the Spirit is from him. But I do not know how the Spirit is from him. . . . Will we be inquisitive, then, and meddle with the essence of God? Where are those who say they have attained and possess the fullness of knowledge? The fact is that they have really fallen into the deepest ignorance. For people who say that they have attained the totality of knowledge in the

---

[106] *De Incomprehensibili* 3, 53-59 (Malingrey, p. 190).

[107] *De Incomprehensibili* 2, 348-50 (Malingrey, p. 170).

[108] *De Incomprehensibili* 5, 261-63 (Malingrey, p. 294).

[109] "Is it frozen crystals of ice? Is it a cloud which has become condensed? Is it air which has grown thicker?" (*De Incomprehensibili* 2, 481-83 [Malingrey, p. 180]).

present life are only depriving themselves of perfect knowledge for the life hereafter.[110]

The theophanies of the Old Testament and passages in which angels are said to behold God are not direct knowledge of his essence. Over against the statements of the Seraphim beholding God and the prophet saying "I saw the Lord" is the controlling principle of John 1:18, "No one has ever seen God" which Chrysostom takes to mean "no one knows God in his essence with complete exactness."[111]

The debate between the Neo-Arians and the Neo-Nicene Cappadocians progressively moved into the area of religious language. Given their realistic view of names, the Neo-Arians thought that "Father" was at best an analogous title—if God really were a Father he would be mutable as are fathers when they produce offspring. "Son," on the other hand, does apply to the essence of Christ because he is essentially begotten. Chrysostom, like the Cappadocians before him, applies both "Father" and "Son" to their respective hypostases. In them is found the distinction of hypostases whereas other titles like "God" and "Lord" are common to both hypostases.

> Just as the expression "one Lord" does not exclude the Father from being perfect Lord nor does this title bestow Lordship on the Son alone, so the expression "one God" does not exclude the Son from being true and genuine God, nor does this title show that Godhead belongs only to the Father. That the Son is God and, while still remaining the Son, is God on the same level as the Father becomes clear from the very addition of the word "Father." If this name of God belonged only to the Father and if it could not designate for us another hypostasis but only that first and unbegotten hypostasis, inasmuch as the name "God" can belong to and denote only that hypostasis, the addition of the name "Father" would serve no purpose. . . . So the addition of "Father" [by Paul in 1 Cor. 8:6] was needed to show that he was speaking of the first and unbegotten hypostasis. The name

---

[110] *De Incomprehensibili* 1, 156-71 (Malingrey pp. 110f.).

[111] *De Incomprehensibili* 4, 220-23 (Malingrey, p. 246).

of God would not suffice to show this, since this name is common to him and to the Son. Some names are common to several; others are proper to one. There are common names to show that the essence is exactly the same; there are proper names to characterize what is proper to the hypostases. The names "Father" and "Son" characterize what is proper to the hypostases; the names "God" and "Lord" show what is common. . . . It is clear from Paul's text that the name "God" is not greater than the name "Lord," nor is the name "Lord" inferior to the name "God."[112]

Chrysostom does not enter into the debate concerning whether these titles in particular are fully descriptive of the essences of the Father and the Son or are used analogously. It may be inferred that such fine points were not a significant part of the Anomoeanism encountered by Chrysostom in Antioch and Constantinople in the late fourth and early fifth centuries. Rather, his point is that the names show the proper distinction and the proper consubstantiality of the Father and the Son. The argument runs thus: the names "Lord" and "God" are both proper names of divinity, and since applied to both the Father and the Son, indicate their essential equality.[113]

Not only did the Arians argue that the title "Son" necessarily indicates a distinction of essence between the Father and the Son, but also that if Christ, as the Son, is homoousios with the Father, then we too are homoousios with God because we are called sons as well. Chrysostom responds to this argument by saying the human title is analogous: "The name 'son' belongs to men and it belongs to the Christ. But it belongs to us by analogy; it belongs to Christ in its proper sense. The title 'only begotten' is his alone and belongs to no one else, even by analogy."[114] He also uses against the Arians their own realistic view of language: "You are called a

---

[112] *De Incomprehensibili* 5, 90-119 (Malingrey, pp. 278ff.).

[113] Chrysostom cites those passages which apply Θεός to Christ: Isa. 7:14; Ps. 82:19; Isa. 9:6; Bar. 3:36-38; Rom. 9:5; Eph. 5:5; 2 Tim. 1:10; Tit. 2:13.

[114] *De Incomprehensibili* 4, 257-61 (Malingrey, p. 248).

son, but he is the son. In your case it is only a word; in his, it is a reality."[115]

On the other hand, other words applied to the Son should be taken analogously rather than with every literal implication. The begottenness of the Son is the best example. Whereas the Arians pressed that attribute to every possible inference of derivation, Chrysostom appeals to the unique nature of the begottenness of the Son:

> If [the Father] begot in human fashion, it would be necessary that there be some interval between the one begetting and the begotten, but, since he begets ineffably and as befits God, leave out the words "before" and "after" for these are terms belonging to time, and the Son is the maker of all ages.[116]

Finally, it is the philosophical method of the Arians itself that Chrysostom identifies as their most fundamental mistake. Their logic-chopping is as weak as all other carnal endeavors. As for Christians, "we are ordered to destroy sophistries and not to arm ourselves with them."[117] The simple reason for the avoidance of speculation is the inherent incomprehensibility of many things accepted by faith. While speaking on the prologue of the Gospel of John Chrysostom asks the Arians: "why do you strive contentiously and in vain to compass by your reason this infinite life? It is not possible to do so. Why do you search for the unsearchable? Why do you scrutinize the inscrutable? Why do you seek the incompehensible?"[118] Divine things must not be subjected to "the order prevailing among us" or to "the necessity of nature."[119]

---

[115] Ὑὸς λέγῃ σύ, ἀλλ ἐκεῖνος ἔστιν· ἐνταῦθα ῥῆμα, ἐκεῖ πρᾶγμα. De Incomprehensibili 7, 2 (PG 48, 758).

[116] Hom. in Jn. 7, 1 (PG 59, 63).

[117] De Incomprehensibili 9, 1 (PG 48, 778).

[118] Hom. in Jn. 7, 1 (PG 59, 63).

[119] This was the case in the Arian understanding of the begottenness of the Son. "When a man wrests spiritual things to his own reasoning, he both utters absurdities and seems to be raving and intoxicated, since he is unduly examining

## Exegetical Considerations

The exegetical homilies of Chrysostom provide a significant body of evidence of the Neo-Arian use of Scripture[120] and of the orthodox response. What follows is a representation of the main exegetical texts used by Chrysostom to refute Neo-Arianism, mainly from his homilies on John, in which he was most consciously addressing Arian thought. We will consider first his reply to some of the favorite exegetical arguments of the Neo-Arians, and then his own exegetical arguments.

Chrysostom preached a full fifteen homilies on the prologue of the Gospel of John (1:1-18), the first four of which centered around the sentence of crucial importance to the orthodox: "In the beginning was the Word, and the Word was with God, and the Word was God." "Logos" was used for the Son instead of substance, says Chrysostom, because "it is not possible to say what God is in substance."[121] The Arians said that the Logos is a work of the Creator, and thus a member of the created realm, to which Chrysostom replies: "This Logos, however, is a being, a distinct person, proceeding from the Father himself without alteration [ἀπαθῶς]."[122] The second phrase— "was with God"— contradicts those who would say "the Logos himself was simply a word uttered, or else merely conceived in the mind [τις εἶναι προφορικὸν ἢ ἐνδιάθετον]."[123] Throughout these early homilies Chrysostom explains the concept of Logos so as to oppose a Sabellian lack of distinction between the Logos and its origin on the one side, and an Arian emphasis on derivation and thus subordination of being on the other.

---

the words, beyond what is pleasing to God, and does not accept the deposit of faith" (*Hom. in Jn.* 24, 3 [PG 59, 146]).

[120] A feature of Neo-Arianism that became more developed in its later stages.

[121] *Hom. in Jn.* 2, 4 (PG 59, 34).

[122] *Hom. in Jn.* 4, 1 (PG 59, 47).

[123] *Hom. in Jn.* 3, 3 (PG 59, 40).

He discusses the Arian interpretation of "in the beginning" compared the Johannine phrase to that of Gen. 1:1, where "beginning" is the creation of the heavens and the earth, implying that Jn. 1:1 means no more than that the Logos was with God from the beginning of creation but not from eternity. "Was" also has no necessary reference to eternity.[124] Chrysostom argues that "beginning" and "was" have different meanings when used of God.[125] He says that 1:2, "He was in the beginning with God" (οὗτος ἦν ἐν ἀρχῇ πρὸς τὸν Θεόν), only strengthens the point "that he was as eternal as the Father himself, for the Father was never without the Logos but always God was with God, though each in his own person [ἐν ὑποστάσει μέντοι ἰδίᾳ]."[126]

One final Arian objection from Jn. 1:1 is that the Father is spoken of with the article, but the Son is not (Θεὸς ἦν ὁ λόγος). Chrysostom's response is to quote other New Testament examples which demonstrate that the article may or may not be used with divine names (Tit. 2:13; Rom. 9:5; Phil. 2:6).

Most of the other examples of Arian exegesis in Chrysostom's homilies are based on direct statements of Jesus which suggest a subordination or inferiority to the Father. One obvious case is Jn. 5:19: "The Son can do nothing of himself." Contrary to what the Arians make of this statement, says Chrysostom, the Son cannot be conceived as powerless, for he himself said he had the power, among other things, to lay down his own life and to take it up again. Additionally, "of himself" in this text and elsewhere can just as easily mean "independently." The meaning of Christ's

---

[124] In this connection, Chrysostom says the Arians used 1 Sam. 1:1 "There was a man from Ramathaimsophim," as an example of the simple use of "was" with no eternal meaning.

[125] The argument is circular unless the third phrase, "and the Logos was God," can be assumed to mean the Logos was fully divine, which, of course, Chrysostom will argue.

[126] *Hom. in Jn.* 4, 1 (PG 59, 47). The Arians insist that "was" means being created, and to back their point, use Acts 2:36 which says God "made (ἐποίησεν) him Lord and Christ." Chrysostom responds by saying the act of "making" applies to the incarnation, not eternal being. *Hom. in Jn.* 3, 3 (PG 59, 41).

words is "It is impossible and inconceivable for me to do anything in contradiction to my Father."[127] Thus the statement is actually a reinforcement of the equality of the Son and the Father rather than its negation.

Chrysostom gives a similar explanation for Jesus' saying that he seeks not his own will but the will of the one who had sent him (e.g. Jn. 6:38). "He meant nothing else than that it is impossible for him to will anything else than what the Father wills."[128]

Jesus' statements about being sent from the Father (e.g. Jn. 5:24) also suggested to the Arians a necessary distinction of essence. In other words, "How can he who sends and he who is sent be of the same substance?"[129] Chrysostom says that such sayings were Christ's way of showing that there is a distinction between the begetter and the begotten, but not a distinction of substance: "All these things were said for no other reason than that we might know of that first cause, and that we might not fall into the error of Sabellius." The same Father-Son, not Creator-Creature distinction is made when Christ says he has been given things by the Father:

> Do you see how their equality is shown and that they differ in one respect only, namely, that one is the Father, while the other is the Son? The expression "he has given" implies this distinction only, and shows that all the other attributes are equal and without difference. From this it is clear that he does everything with as much authority and power as the Father and is not endowed with power from some outside source, for he has life as the Father has.[130]

Certainly one of the most pertinent texts in Arian exegesis is Jn. 14:28: "If you loved me, you would rejoice that I am going to the Father, for the Father is greater than I (ὁ πατὴρ μείζων μού ἐστιν)." It is interesting that Chrysostom does not explain this text

---

[127] *Hom. in Jn.* 38, 4 (PG 59, 217).

[128] *Hom. in Jn.* 39, 4 (PG 59, 225).

[129] *Hom. in Jn.* 39, 2 (PG 59, 221).

[130] *Hom. in Jn.* 39, 3 (PG 59, 223).

on the basis of the incarnate nature of Christ, nor by distinguishing his human nature from the divine. He allows that there is some sense in which the eternal Father can be called greater than the eternal Son, especially in the language used for the benefit of the first, unenlightened, disciples: "But, if someone should assert that the Father is 'greater' insofar as he is the begetter of the Son, we shall not contradict this. However, this, to be sure, does not cause the Son to be of another substance."[131]

These, then, are some of the ways in which Chrysostom responded to the exegetical interpretations of the Arians. On the other side, there are many occasions in the homilies on John for Chrysostom to positively assert the equality of the Father and the Son. At one point, he lists a whole string of statements that, by comparing the Father and the Son in being and in operation, indicate their essential oneness:

> "I am in the Father and the Father in me"; and ". . .he who sees me sees also the Father" [Jn. 14:11, 9]; and "that all men may honor the Son even as they honor the Father"; "As the Father raises the dead and gives them life, even so the Son also gives life to whom he will"; "My Father works even until now, and I work" [Jn. 5:23, 21, 17]; "Even as the Father knows me and I know the Father" [Jn. 10:15]; "I and the Father are one" [Jn. 10:30]. And everywhere, by putting "as" and "so" and "being one with the Father," he made clear his complete equality with him [τὴν πρὸς αὐτὸν ἀπαραλλαξίαν δηλοῖ].[132]

So also when Jesus said "he who believes in me, believes not in me but in him who sent me" (Jn. 12:44), he was speaking of "the complete identity of their substance."[133]

Chrysostom often specifies what aspect of equality is indicated by the activities and sayings of Christ, that is, the essential qualities or activities of deity shared by the Father and

---

[131] *Hom. in Jn.* 75, 4 (PG 59, 408).

[132] *Hom. in Jn.* 3, 4 (PG 59, 42-43).

[133] *Hom. in Jn.* 69, 1 (PG 59, 377).

the Son. There is a summary of those specifics in a comment in the seventh homily on the incomprehensible nature of God:

> When he wishes to show that his essence [τῆς οὐσίας] is in no way different from the Father's, he says: "He who has seen me has seen the Father." When he wishes to show that his power [τῆς δυνάμεως] is equal to the Father's, he says: "For as the Father raises the dead and grants life, so the Son also grants life to those whom he wishes." When he wishes to show that he is to receive identical worship [τῆς λατρείας] with the Father, he says: "So that all men may honor the Son just as they honor the Father." And when he wishes to show he has the same authority [τὴν αὐθεντίαν] to amend the law, he says: "My Father works, and I work." But these heretics ignore all these texts. They do not understand the name "Son" in its proper meaning. . . .[134]

The equality of the Father and the Son consists in the sameness of essence, of power, of worship, and of authority. Throughout his homilies Chrysostom frequently repeats these and other attributes of equality like glory, honor, dignity, truth, works, operation, will. These terms refer both to the inherent attributes of deity (essence, glory, dignity, honor, authority, truth, will) and to the effects of the divine character in the world (power, works, operation).

The most telling passages concerning the consubstantiality of the Son with the Father according to Chrysostom are those which indicate the Son's activity in this world and in the future—the oneness of power, authority, and thus, glory and honor of the Father and the Son. For example, Jn. 5:21-23: "Just as the Father raises the dead and gives them life, even so the Son also gives life to whom he wishes; for not even the Father judges any one, but he has given all judgment to the Son, in order that all may honor the Son, even as they honor the Father," shows the complete identity of power and will of the Son with the Father:

> He both does all that the Father does, and also does it in the manner in which the Father does it. Whether you mention

---

[134] De Incomprehensibili 7, 2 (PG 48, 758).

resurrection from the dead, or creation of bodies, or forgiveness of sins, or anything else whatsoever, he does it in the same way as his Father.[135]

The clear implication of such sameness of activity is a sameness of honor and glory: "The honor of the Son is bound up with the honor of the Father.... There is identity of his substance and glory."[136]

The eschatological works of the Son, as identified in Jn. 6:44, "and I will raise him up on the last day," also indicate an identity of dignity and power with the Father:

> In this text the Son has no inconsiderable dignity, for if, to be sure, the Father draws men, the Son it is who raises them up, not, of course, separating his works from those of the Father (for how could that be?), but showing that their power is the same.[137]

Likewise, the ability to save, to grant freedom from sin ("if therefore the Son makes you free, you shall be free indeed" [Jn.8:36]) shows the Son's "consubstantiality with his Father and ... [that he has] the same authority as his Father."[138] When Jesus answered the disciples' query about the man blind from birth, Jesus' reply, that the man was blind that the glory of God may be manifest (Jn. 9:2), referred to his own glory as God. In the healing and the forgiveness of the man's sins Jesus was doing "not similar works, but the same ones" as the Father.[139] And when Jesus described himself as the good shepherd, saying of his sheep, "I give eternal life to them, and they shall never perish, and no one shall snatch them out of my hand.... I and the Father are one" (Jn. 10:28-30), he was indicating an identity of power with the Father which must mean an identity of substance. Finally, we note

---

[135] *Hom. in Jn.* 38, 4 (PG 59, 218).

[136] *Hom. in Jn.* 39, 2 (PG 59, 221).

[137] *Hom. in Jn.* 46, 1 (PG 59, 258).

[138] *Hom. in Jn.* 54, 2 (PG 59, 298).

[139] *Hom. in Jn.* 56, 2 (PG 59, 308).

Chrysostom's explanation why the consubstantiality of the Son was revealed through all these significant but indirect evidences: "Since it was not possible to see his substance, by means of the sameness and identity of their works he furnished proof of the equality of their power."[140] That the Son's equality with the Father was revealed by his works rather than through some direct disclosure of his substance was simply due to the incomprehensibility of the divine essence.

Chrysostom's exegetical approach in defense of the full divinity of Christ concentrates both on the disputation of Arian exegesis and on the identification of texts that either directly state the oneness of the Father and the Son or that imply such by the description of activities possible and appropriate only for divinity. This last type of text is important because the seemingly direct statements of identity (such as: "I and the Father are one") all could be explained by the Arians as a dynamic rather than essential unity.

The polemic against Neo-Arianism was not the only context in which Chrysostom discussed the divinity of Christ. In particular, the prominence of the Jewish population, especially in Antioch, is to be noted in this connection.[141] On at least two occasions Chrysostom directly addressed the Jews or the judaizing Christians of Antioch.[142] However, while these polemical and apologetic writings do discuss the divinity of Christ, they include

---

[140] *Hom. in Jn.* 61, 2 (PG 59, 339).

[141] See Robert L. Wilken, *John Chrysostom and the Jews: Rhetoric and Reality in the Late 4th Century* (Berkeley: U. of California, 1983); Wayne Meeks and Robert L. Wilken, *Jews and Christians in Antioch in the First Four Centuries of the Common Era* (Missoula, Mont.: Scholars' Press, 1978); Paul Harkins, "Chrysostom the Apologist: On the Divinity of Christ," in P. Granfield and J. A. Jungmann, eds., *Kyriakon: Festschrift Johannes Quasten*, 2 vols. (Münster Westf.: Aschendorff, 1970) 1:441-51.

[142] See his eight Discourses *Against Judaizing Christians*, trans. Paul Harkins, FC, vol. 68 (Washington, D. C., 1979); and the *Demonstration Against Jews and Pagans that Christ is God*, trans. Paul Harkins, FC, vol. 73 (Washington, D. C., 1985).

no theological discussions of the divine nature, but only proofs of divinity based on fulfillment of prophecy and miracles.

## Summary

We have thus far considered only the first question of Christology—that of the deity of the Son. What follow are some preliminary conclusions about that one aspect before we consider the subsequent issues of the humanity of Christ and the relationship of the natures.

1. Chrysostom's understanding of the deity of the Son reflects the conclusions reached at Nicaea (325) and Constantinople (381). Without explicitly referring to either council, Chrysostom builds upon their conclusions as evidenced in the terms he uses: the Son is *homoousios* with the Father, and their distinction is one of *hypostasis*.

2. Regarding religious language, Chrysostom admits a limited use of terms regarding substance. *Ousia* and *hypostasis*, words which some, like the Homoeans, rejected as being too unbiblical and misleading, are acceptable. But the emphasis of the Neo-Arians on generatedness and ungeneratedness is pressing beyond the limits of religious language, and assumes that the divine nature is comprehensible, an assumption which is presumptuous at best and the height of heretical pride at worst. Chrysostom most often uses the biblical terms "Father" and "Son" or "Christ," and, in describing the specific characteristics of the consubtantial divine nature, words like power, honor, and glory.

3. Unlike Basil and Gregory Nazianzus, who each wrote treatises opposing the Neo-Arian Eunomius and his teachings, Chrysostom addressed Anomoeanism in general. Consequently, we get a picture of the popular effects of Anomoeanism rather than a detailed refutation of the thought and writings of its most sophisticated leaders. While it is improbable that Theodosius' decrees against the Neo-Arians caused them to attend the orthodox churches *en masse*, it is obvious that Chrysostom was involved in an ongoing polemical struggle with the Anomoeans

and that at least some of them were attending his preaching. At least in the earlier part of his career, Chrysostom considered Neo-Arianism a live issue, and as a pastor sought both to convert his heretical listeners and to protect the orthodox.

4. Nonetheless, Chrysostom's homilies do show some of the specific exegetical arguments used by the Anomoeans. At least on the evidence of his writings, there does not seem to be much advancement in Arian exegesis. The texts utilized are the obvious choices, already used by earlier generations of Arians. Statements about the Son's adherence to the Father's will and of the Son's doing nothing apart from the Father, says Chrysostom, do not necessarily imply dependence, but simply unity. That the Father sends the Son and gives things into his hand indicates that there is a real distinction between them, but not one of essence.

5. On the other hand, the positive arguments for the full deity of the Son include, but go beyond, the straightforward statements of oneness like "I and the Father are one," and "he who has seen me has seen the Father." Every comparison of the Son and the Father in their works or honor speaks of their consubstantiality. Such evidence was too weak for Anomoeans who expected to be able to answer the question of oneness by a comparison of comprehensible essences. But Chrysostom, like the Cappadocians, disputed the assumption that the essences are knowable. The reason the comparison of works and honor is adequate is that they are the realities closest to essence that the human mind can comprehend. Essence itself—be it of God or ourselves—is inherently incomprehensible.

If in his teaching on the deity of Christ Chrysostom was maintaining the much-discussed conclusions of past conciliar settlements, what he said about the humanity of Christ—to which we turn next—involved new questions about what the long-held doctrine of the fullness of the humanity of the incarnate Son might entail.

# Chapter Three

# Chrysostom on
# the Humanity of Christ

## *The Emotional Experience of Jesus*

We turn next to the specific content of Chrysostom's understanding of the humanity of Christ. Needless to say, in a corpus so large, comments on the issues involved abound. Our approach will be to consider first Chrysosom's teaching on the commonly understood operations of human nature: emotion, intellect, and will; and then to turn to his more explicit explanations of the human nature of Christ as flesh and soul.

To the Greeks the impassibility of the divine was necessary because any god who is subject to the same whims and power of human emotion as ordinary human beings is a god more controlled than in control. The ἀπάθεια of God is the assurance that there is something beyond the fickleness of life seen in the endless cycles of birth and death of the human race. Thus Gregory of Nyssa says: "In our faith we introduce no element of weakness [πάθος] in our ideas of God."[143] To do so would be to admit into the Godhead the principle by which human beings choose evil instead of virtue, and the possibility of alteration or change.

That presents Christianity with a serious challenge to its own consistency, however. How can it be true that the unchangeable

---

[143] *Oratio catechetica* 16, trans. C. Richardson, in *Christology of the Later Fathers*, ed. E. R. Hardy (Philadelphia: Westminster, 1954), p. 292.

God has saved the race by taking on a human form that by its very nature is subject to πάθος and is continually changing? Gregory puts the question this way:

> With what, then, does our religion contend the divine came into contact? Was it weakness (πάθος) in its strict sense, that is, evil, or was it the changing movement of nature? Were our teaching to affirm that the divine entered a state which is morally forbidden it would be our duty to avoid such a preposterous doctrine, implying, as it does, an unsound view of the divine nature.[144]

He illustrates the point by saying that a doctor who comes to treat a disease comes into contact with the sickness, but remains free from the weakness or suffering (πάθος) that comes from it. The shortcoming of Gregory's illustration is that the incarnation as understood by the Greek Fathers is more than a visit to the side of the bed of the afflicted. It is, to extend Gregory's metaphor, getting into the same bed, indeed, into the same body, as the one who is ill.

The question of the degree to which Christ was a participant in human passion and how that may be consistent with an impassible divine nature arises at several key points in Chrysostom's homilies on the gospels. In particular, we will consider three passages that raise the issue explicitly: the incident of the raising of Lazarus, Jesus' expression of anxiety over his impending death, and Jesus' agony in the garden of Gethsemane.

## The Raising of Lazarus

The fourth gospel perhaps more than the others relates incidents of unusual emotional intensity. When Chrysostom reaches the story of the raising of Lazarus he encounters a pericope with an interesting backgound (Jesus' special relationship with Martha, Mary, and Lazarus) and one that includes the rare occurrence of Jesus being "troubled," and, what is even more

---

[144] *Oratio catechetica* 16.

unusual, of his weeping. Chrysostom explains what was happening in Christ:

> In order to confirm the fact of his human nature, he wept a little and put off the miracle for the present. . . . In order that he might not lose the quarry [the witnessing crowd] he even displayed a characteristic of human nature, for he wept and was troubled. For he knew that grief arouses sympathy. Next, having curbed his own display of emotion [πάθος] (for the words: "He groaned in Spirit" means this—that he outwardly restrained his troubled feelings), he asked the following question: "Where have you laid him?" And so, the question was asked without any outward manifestation of his grief [ὀλοφυρμός]. . . . He came, then, to the tomb and again he curbed his emotion [πάθος]. But why in the world was it that the Evangelist was at great pains to mention repeatedly that he wept and that he groaned? That you might learn that he truly did assume our nature [ἀληθῶς τὴν φύσιν τὴν ἡμετέραν περιεβάλετο].[145]

Chrysostom sees John as ordinarily concentrating on the divinity of the Son, but here, as speaking of Christ's "human nature in a much more humble strain."

Whenever an expression of human emotion is attributed to Christ, Chrysostom is eager to point out the purpose of it.[146] That in itself betrays the fact that Chrysostom assumes that any emotion that can be predicated of Christ must ultimately be under his control. Lack of control in the human race is what binds it to its own evil habits, but the salvation provided by Christ includes the restoration of self-discipline. The purpose of Christ's weeping and being troubled at the tomb of Lazarus is to prove "his human nature" (τὴν ἀνθρωπίνην φύσιν).[147] At one and the same time,

---

[145] *Hom. in Jn.* 63, 1 (PG 59, 350).

[146] "If he were not truly possessed of our human nature (εἰ μὴ τῆς φύσεως ἦν τῆς ἡμετέρας), he would not have been overcome by grief once and then again a second time" (*Hom. in Jn.* 63, 2 [PG 59, 350]).

[147] Chrysostom's statement: ἀληθῶς τὴν φύσιν τὴν ἡμετέραν περιεβάλετο includes the verb περιβάλλω, a favorite description throughout the patristic period for the relationship between soul and body, and, in particular, the

then, Christ demonstrated his divinity in one of his greatest miracles, but only after he had revealed the πάθος that even he possessed. Chrysostom links the present passage with the Passion of Christ, especially as described in the other gospels where agony and sweat further attest to the "genuineness of the incarnation" (ἀλήθεια τῆς οἰκονομίας).

Chrysostom does not explain away this occasion of emotion in the life of Christ; indeed, he uses a variety of words to describe it. If his discussion makes the event seem somewhat contrived it is because he will not allow a truly spontaneous activity of Christ on a human level. That would make Christ subject to a tendency that has its source in his humanity and contradict the belief that in the incarnation God superseded all human changeableness. The divine nature remains in control. There is only one subject here—not the Logos imitating a human response, nor an assumed man acting out the necessary consequences of his own limited psyche—but rather, Christ conceived as a unified Person.[148]

His πάθος was genuine, but not abundant: "He wept a little."[149] Here is the monk speaking of moderation. Christ may display some grief or anger or anguish, but, in excess, πάθος is weakness, and weakness is associated with moral failure. In this same connection, a passage from the seventy-eighth homily on Matthew contains a description of the overall limits of Christ's πάθος with a view to encouraging similar control in the Christian:

> Should you fall into grief, take heed lest the tyranny of despondency pervert your tongue, but that you speak like

---

relationship between the Logos and the flesh of Christ. See, for example, Athanasius *Orationes contra Arianos* 2, 74 (PG 26, 305).

[148] Chrysostom acknowledges the human nature, but does not sense a necessity to hold it distinct from the divine nature. Compare this with Leo's comment on the raising of Lazarus: "It is not an act of one and the same nature to weep over a friend's death in an access of pity and to summon that very friend back to life" (Leo I's letter to Flavian of Constantinople, trans. in Norris, *The Christological Controversy*, p. 151).

[149] Cf. *Hom. in Matt.* 66, 2 (PG 58, 628): "setting measures of sorrow, when he had need to mourn, he weeps moderately."

Christ. For he too mourned [ἐπένθησε] for Lazarus and Judas. Should you fall into fear, seek again to speak even as he. For he himself fell into fear for your sake, with regard to the economy [κατὰ τὸν τῆς οἰκονομίας λόγον]. Also say, "Nevertheless, not as I will, but as you will." And if you should lament, weep calmly as He. Should you fall into plots and sorrows, treat these too as Christ. For indeed he had plots laid against him, and was in sorrow, and said, "My soul is exceeding sorrowful, even unto death." And all the examples he presented to you, in order that you should continually observe the same measures, and not destroy the rules that have been given you. So you will. . . maintain the limits [τὰ μέτρα] he observed in despondency [ἀθυμίᾳ], in anger [ὀργῇ], in suffering [πένθει], in agony [ἀγωνίᾳ].[150]

Here again genuine human emotion is attributed to Christ, but with the limitations that the divinity of Christ brings to bear upon it. The examples represent a considerable breadth of emotions, from mourning and sorrow in reaction to Lazarus' death and Judas' apostasy, to the fear that accompanied his own death. Of the four words in the last phrase, three certainly describe the Passion—despondency, suffering, and agony—while the fourth probably recalls Christ's righteous indignation in the cleansing of the temple. The emotions were real, not feigned, but they were not untamed. Christ's control in such situations provides a model by which the Christian can "maintain the limits" in similar fashion.

One final detail of interest in this section is the statement: "He himself fell into fear for your sake, with regard to the economy" [ἐνέπεσε γὰρ καὶ αὐτὸς εἰς φόβον διά σε κατὰ τὸν τῆς οἰκονομίας λόγον]. Christ's falling into fear was on our account, and in that lies the broader principle of the incarnation. Occurences of πάθος in Christ, in other words, are not incidental to the incarnation, but represent its central achievement—identification with human nature and experience.

---

[150] *Hom. in Matt.* 78, 4 (PG 58, 716).

## Jesus' Fear of Death

Chrysostom pauses deliberately when, in the Gospel of John, he comes to Jesus' statement "Now my soul is troubled" (12:27). In its context Jesus is describing his death as a grain of wheat that is fruitful only after it dies and is buried. Lazarus has just been raised, the triumphal entry is imminent. Jesus asks: "And what shall I say? 'Father, save me from this hour?' No, for this purpose I have come to this hour." Here is a gospel saying descriptive of Jesus' feelings about the passion as well as its purpose. Chrysostom comments:

> Lest they might assert that he was altogether free from human pain [τῶν ὠδίων] and so found it easy to accept death, and that he gave us encouragement without himself being in any danger of death, he showed that, even though he dreaded [ἀγωνιῶν] death, he did not refuse to undergo it, because of its efficacy for our salvation. And this is of the economy, not of the divinity. That is why he said: "Now my soul is troubled" (for, if this were not so, what connection was there between this statement and the following one: "Father, save me from this hour"?) And he was so deeply troubled [τετάρακται] that he even sought release if it were possible to escape. This was the weakness [τὰ ἀσθενήματα] of the human nature. . . . This very effectually shows that he was human and that the nature did not wish to suffer death, but was clinging to the present life, and it proves that he was not without human feelings [οὐκ ἔξω τῶν ἀνθρωπίνων παθῶν ἦν]. Just as the fact that he suffered hunger was not held against him, or that he slept, so the fact that he dreaded [ἐφίεσθαι] the separation from this present life ought not to be held against him, either. Christ's body [σῶμα] was, to be sure, altogether free from sin, but it was not without physical needs [φυσικῶν ἀναγκῶν], otherwise, it would not have been a real body.[151]

Here again Chrysostom depicts pain, fear, and anguish as real experiences of the incarnate Christ. His vocabulary is varied so as to reinforce the point, including the use of "weakness" as a

---

[151] *Hom. in Jn.* 67, 1-2 (PG 59, 371).

description of the human nature.[152] There is less emphasis on the
event being a conscious demonstration than in the previous
passage, although it is hardly depicted as a truly spontaneous
response. The showing of emotion is still a didactic device by
which Christ is consciously proving that he was not without
human πάθος and thus that he was genuinely human. But is
Chrysostom describing a full and complete human nature acting
out its ordinary impulses? He says, "this is of the economy, not of
the divinity,"[153] which is not necessarily a distinction between a
human and a divine nature in Christ (a point to which we shall
have to return in a later section).

Finally, it must be noted that this experience of human πάθος
in Christ is associated with purely physical experiences like
hunger and sleep, and that Chrysostom uses σῶμα toward the end
of the section as if it were the seat of human emotion.[154] The point
is significant because if the emotions Chrysostom discusses are
simply an extension of the body, then the human nature of Christ
at least as regards πάθος would have much less significance than if
it experienced emotions that had their origin in the soul.[155] To put
it another way, πάθος as a natural aspect of the body is much

---

[152] Although note Chrysostom's discussion of 2 Cor. 13:4 "He [Christ] was
crucified in ἀσθένεια," words that have "much obscurity" and mean the humility
experienced by anyone under persecution or distress, not in any sense a weakness
of nature (*Hom. in 2 Cor.* 29, 2).

[153] ταῦτα δὲ τῆς οἰκονομίας, οὐ τῆς θεότητος.

[154] Christ's body had φυσικαὶ ἀνάγκαι, natural needs, i.e. the reactions any
ordinary human body would have. Cf. Chrysostom's discussion of Jesus' prophecy
about Peter's destiny, in particular, that he would be martyred unwillingly:
"Then, what is the meaning of 'where you would not'? He was referring to the
feelings of our nature and to the necessity of the flesh [τῆς σαρκὸς ἀνάγκην] and
how the soul is unwillingly torn away from the body" (*Hom. in Jn.* 88, 1 [PG 59,
479]). Here, as in the passage under discussion, the πάθος that arises out of
suffering is a natural, even necessary, reaction of the flesh or body.

[155] Cf. Camillus Hay who does draw the conclusion that for Chrysostom
Christ's dread of death is simply the principle of self-preservation which is a
natural aspect of any human body ("Integrity of the Human Nature," p. 309).

more a description of the lower, or fleshly, soul than the rational soul.

## The Agony in the Garden

There is no other gospel passage that Chrysostom examines more for its christological significance than that of the agony in the garden. He makes extended comments on the incident in the eighty-third homily on Matthew, in the seventh homily in the series *On the Incomprehensible Nature of God*, and in the sermon, *In illud: Pater si possibile est.* The prayer in Gethsemane is a problem for a variety of reasons: if the Son of God was one with the Father, how could his will have any degree of variation from the will of the Father, indeed, how could he have a will of his own in any sense? And, how could the Son of God, even if true man, be so overcome by his impending death that his emotion nearly overwhelms him? The question of opposing wills will come up in a later section, but with regard to the second issue, we see Chrysostom defending the genuineness of Christ's humanity on account of the anguish he experienced.

> How is it, then, that in his prayer he says: "If it be possible?" He is showing the weakness which belongs to a human nature [τῆς ἀνθρωπίνης φύσεως τὴν ἀσθένειαν]. And human nature would prefer not to be torn from the present life; it would draw back and shrink from death. Why? Because God has implanted in human nature a love for the life of this world. Even after he had said so many things of this sort, some men still made so bold as to maintain that Christ had not assumed flesh [ὅτι σάρκα οὐκ ἀνέλαβεν]. . . . If the flesh does not wish to die, it should not be condemned. To shun death is according to its nature. And Christ gives abundant proof of every aspect of his human nature—except sin. And he did this so as to block up the mouths of the heretics. Therefore, when he says: "If it be possible, let this cup pass from me" and "Not as I will but as you will," he is showing nothing other than that he is clothed in flesh [σάρκα ἀληθῶς περιβέβληται], and that the flesh fears death. For it is a mark of the flesh that it fears death, shrinks back from it, and struggles against it. At that time, he left his flesh deserted and stripped of any divine power of operation to

show its weakness [τὴν ἀσθένειαν] and to confirm its nature. At other times, he conceals it so that you may know that he is not merely a man.[156]

There is no scandal at all, then, even if Christ's agony is genuine, for it is attributable to his true flesh whose ordinary nature it is to seek life instead of death. The quality is amoral, a "weakness," that was countered by the overwhelming divine impulse in Christ. This weakness is evidence of Christ's "clothing." The interesting expression "at that time he left it [his flesh] deserted and stripped of its characteristic operation" (νῦν μὲν οὖν ἐρήμην αὐτὴν ἀφίησι, καὶ γυμνὴν τῆς οἰκείας ἐνεργείας), properly rendered by the translator as "divine power of operation," points to a kenosis brought about voluntarily—and one that is temporary. Kenosis in the garden is the Son's way of communicating the genuineness of his flesh, and consequently, the reality of his sacrificial death to any would-be docetists. But "at other times" the tendencies of flesh recede to the background as the divine ἐνέργεια is demonstrated fully.

Another entire homily[157] is devoted to the Gethsemane scene, where Chrysostom returns to many of the same themes:

> For this reason, just as he hungered, as he slept, as he felt fatigue, as he ate and drank, so also did he deprecate death, thereby manifesting his humanity, and that weakness of human nature [τὴν ἀσθένειαν τῆς φύσεως] which does not submit without pain [ἀπαθῶς] to be torn from this present life. For had he not uttered any of these things, it might have been said that if he were a man he ought to have experienced human feelings [παθεῖν τὰ ἀνθρώπου]. And what are these? In the case of one about to be crucified, fear and agony, and pain in being torn from this present life. For a sense of the charm which surrounds present things is implanted in human nature. On this account, wishing to prove the reality of the fleshly clothing [ἀληθῆ τῆς σαρκὸς τὴν περιβολὴν], and to give assurance of the

---

[156] *De Incomprehensibili* 7, 6 (PG 48, 766).

[157] *In illud: Pater si possibile est*, trans. in NPNF 1st ser., 9:201-07. There are no internal clues to indicate the date or circumstance of the homily.

incarnation, he manifests the naked feelings [τὰ πάθη γυμνὰ] of man with full demonstration.[158]

Once again, it is the proper weakness of the flesh, to Christ a clothing, which produces fear, agony, and pain at the prospect of being cut off from the present life. As in the last passage, the "nakedness" of the emotional expression of Jesus suggests the clear distinction Chrysostom made between the humanity of Christ and Christ considered as a whole acting subject.[159]

What, then, are we to conclude Chrysostom understood of Christ's incarnate nature in the light of the gospel accounts of his human πάθος? First, that the expressions should be taken as genuinely human. Yet Chrysostom is not eager to find many indicators of such raw human πάθος in the incarnate Christ. He discusses the issue only when it has to be explained, and the form that his teaching takes at those points is always slightly apologetic. Of course, it may be that such passages were problematic for Chrysostom because they were problematic for everybody—for Docetists and Manichees testimonies so vividly human that they were seen to be indicative of an only apparent humanity in Christ, for Arians so ordinary that they were proof of his creatureliness. And if from no other corner, at least from Chrysostom's congregation itself, pressing questions must have come in course about how he who saves human beings from the mundane could seem himself to be subject to it.[160]

There are other gospel sayings which Chrysostom could have used as further evidence of the reality of Christ's emotional

---

[158] *In illud: Pater si possibile est* 4 (PG 51, 38).

[159] Chrysostom's discussion of the same incident in his eighty-third homily on Matthew contains no features beyond the passages already examined, nor does one final comment on Gethsemane in the eighty-fifth homily on John.

[160] Note some of the opening words of *In illud: Pater si possibile est*: "For I imagine that many feel perplexed as to the reason why these words were uttered by Christ, and it is probable also that any heretics who are present may pounce upon the words, and thereby upset many of the more simple-minded brethren" (*In illud: Pater si possibile est* 1 [PG 51, 31]).

experience but does not, for example, the indignation shown in the cleansing of the temple and the frequent occasions on which Christ was overcome with compassion. Chrysostom deals with the reactions of Christ on a human level only when he has to.

The lesson he always derives from such passages is how redeemed human beings can themselves learn discipline and control over their own agonies and griefs. Life is best lived above the passions, as Christ demonstrated when insulted by scribes and Pharisees or praised by the multitudes. He "is superior to either passion. . . neither at the one time moved to anger, nor at the other softened by flattery."[161]

While such moralistic interpretations of the expressed passions of Christ may seem consistent with the view that Christ possessed a free and self-conscious center of human emotion, Chrysostom's own understanding stops short of that. The association of grief and agony with the self-preserving defenses of the σῶμα is less than a description of a freely-reacting soul in Christ. Chrysostom chose a different explanation than did Theodore of Mopsuestia. Such experiences are not the "assumed man" acting naturally and spontaneously out of his own distinct nature. It was the Lord, as man, who allowed the reality of his fleshly clothing to be shown in the exercising of its own cringing reaction to threat.

On the other hand, it would be hasty to compare Chrysostom to the likes of Apollinaris on this point. Even though Christ's divine nature dominated emotion, Chrysostom still insists on his genuine humanity. And it is not only an instinct of self-preservation that is described.[162] In the case of Christ's grief at the tomb of Lazarus self-preservation is not the issue. Chrysostom

---

[161] *Hom. in Matt.* 43, 1 (PG 57, 457).

[162] While Hay has rightly concluded that the Gethsemane explanations link emotion with the body's defense of itself, that is not the only kind of emotion displayed by Christ as Chrysostom sees it. Note other kinds of emotions in *Hom. in Heb.* 15, 4 (PG 63, 122).: "He was sad indeed oftentimes. For even when he looked on Jerusalem, he wept, and when he thought on the traitor he was troubled, and when he was about to raise Lazarus, he wept."

does not thoroughly explore why, humanly speaking, Christ would display grief at the tomb, but nevertheless he takes it at face value as a genuine expression. We are presented, then, with a faculty in Christ that reacts to the world in limited instances in the way any ordinary human would, but its reaction is never beyond the control of the divine ἐνέργεια which dominates the earthly life of Christ.[163]

## *Intellectual Activity in Christ*

Another faculty of the human soul—intellect—presented the Fathers with a difficult set of christological questions at least from the time Apollinaris started asking them. If Christ possessed a full human nature, did he think humanly in a way that was distinct from his divine nature? Someone who is primarily an exegete and homilist may have more reason than most to affirm such, since the gospel accounts present several examples of limitation of intellectual perception in the person of Jesus. However, Chrysostom allows no such understanding of the passages. If kenosis occurred in any sense in the incarnation, it was not on the level of knowing.

Minor examples of Chrysostom's approach include incidents in which Jesus asks a question. When he asked Philip what he had in his hand "surely he was not ignorant of what he [Philip] would say."[164] Similarly, a question to the blind man healed in Jn. 9, "Do you believe in the Son of God?," was asked not because Jesus needed to know, but to give the man opportunity to profess his faith.[165]

---

[163] Frances Young points out that the ideal of ἀπάθεια was so basic to fourth and fifth century philosophical currents that it was not at all uncommon to find among Christians the view that while Christ's flesh suffered on the cross, the Logos remained unaffected, a view often called docetic in modern interpretations but unfairly so. "A Reconsideration of Alexandrian Christology," *J Eccl H* 22 (1971), pp. 112ff.

[164] *Hom. in Jn.* 42, 1 (PG 59, 240).

[165] *Hom. in Jn.* 59, 1 (PG 59, 322).

Any situation that Jesus appeared to happen upon unknowingly is also thoroughly explained. Matthew and Luke record that Jesus came up to the fig tree because he was hungry, but it is only the disciples' assumption that the Evangelists are recording when they say that Jesus thought there would be figs on it.[166] Crucifixion is not ordinarily approached knowingly, but in Christ's case he came to it "not in ignorance, nor by constraint."[167]

Here again, the words in Gethsemane present Chrysostom with evidence of the humility of Christ, but could they really mean that Christ did not know whether or not he would actually have to face the cross? The statement: "if it be possible" in any ordinary use of language would imply contingency, but Chrysostom rejects such a possibility in Christ's case.

> "Father if it be possible take away the cross." What do you say? Is he ignorant whether this be possible or impossible? Who would venture to say this? Yet the words are those of one who is ignorant. For the addition of the word "if," is indicative of doubt, but as I said we must not attend to the words merely, but turn our attention to the sense, and learn the aim of the speaker, and the cause and the occasion, and by putting all these things together turn out the hidden meaning. The unspeakable Wisdom, then, who knows the Father even as the Father knows the Son, how should he have been ignorant of this? For this knowledge concerning his passion was not greater than the knowledge concerning his essential nature [τῆς γνώσεως τῆς περὶ οὐσίας], which he alone accurately knew. "For as the Father knows me" he says "even so know I the Father." And why do I speak of the only begotten Son of God? For even the prophets appear not to have been ignorant of this fact, but to have known it clearly, and to have declared beforehand with much assurance that so it must come to pass, and would certainly be.[168]

---

[166] *Hom. in Matt.* 67, 1 (PG 58, 633).

[167] *Hom. in Matt.* 65, 1 (PG 58, 647).

[168] *In illud: Pater si possibile est* 1 (PG 51, 31-32).

Chrysostom goes on to elucidate other sayings of Jesus that indicate that he came to his passion in full knowledge of its salvific and historical necessity. Why else, for instance, would Jesus have rebuked Peter for insisting that suffering and humiliation were inappropriate for the Son of God?

But besides the sayings in the gospels, Chrysostom has another major reason for not being able to accept ignorance in Christ even in his incarnate state, namely, the basic philosophical assumption that absolute Wisdom encompasses all knowledge, and Christ is that Wisdom. Knowledge is central to the Greek conception of deity. There is nothing unusual in the assumption that omniscience is an attribute of divine nature. For the Greek Fathers σοφία was as adequate a description of the divinity of Christ as λόγος.[169] What is significant here is that Chrysostom does not allow ignorance in any sense to be associated even with the incarnate state of Christ. Whereas passion could be an experience of Christ "according to the economy," lack of knowledge is too far removed from the essence of divinity for it to be posited of the Son under any circumstances. Neither is an appeal made here to a distinct human nature that has its own natural limitations. Seeming incidents of ignorance in Christ are explained by the circumstance and the didactic intention of Christ, not by any ontological considerations.

The most problematic passage for Chrysostom in this regard, and indeed for all the Greek Fathers, is the one in which the Son of Man is said to be ignorant of the coming day of judgment: "No one knows about that day or hour, not even the angels in heaven, nor the Son, but only the Father" (Mk. 13:32). Even before explaining the sense of the statement, Chrysostom rejects any interpretation of real ignorance in Christ:

> When will he know it? Will it be together with us? But who would say this? And the Father he knows clearly, even as clearly as he knows the Son; and of the day is he ignorant? Moreover, "the Spirit indeed searches even the deep things of

---

[169] Note 1 Cor. 1:24: Χριστὸν Θεοῦ δύναμιν καὶ Θεοῦ σοφίαν.

God," and does not he know so much as the time of the judgment? But how he ought to judge he knows, and of the secrets of each he has a full perception; and what is far more common than that, of this could he be ignorant? And how, if "all things were made by him, and without him was not even one thing made," was he ignorant of the day? For he who made the worlds, it is quite plain that he made the times also; and if the times, even that day. How then is he ignorant of that which he made?[170]

The Son knows with clarity and distinctness [σαφῶς] what exists on both sides of the line between Creator and creation. There is no way, then, that Christ is even imitating humanity in making such a statement. Chrysostom is directly addressing listeners sympathetic to Eunomius when he goes on to say that it is ridiculous to assume one can know the substance of the Son and not allow that he knows the day of judgment. "Neither do you know what God is in his substance, though ten thousand times you talk thus madly, nor is the Son ignorant of the day, but is even in full certainty of it."[171] He then carefully highlights just how clearly Christ shows his explicit knowledge of the judgment, and concludes that Christ's language here is purposely extreme so as to discourage speculation about "times and seasons." In other words, by associating knowledge of the day of judgment with the Father, Christ was telling his listeners just how wide the gap is between their knowledge and God's.[172]

In summary, Chrysostom consistently interprets the gospel passages attributing ignorance to Christ as anything but ignorance. There is nothing in Chrysostom's observations on the gospels or in

---

[170] *Hom. in Matt.* 77, 1 (PG 58, 703).

[171] *Hom. in Matt.* 77, 2 (PG 58, 703).

[172] It is important to note another explanation that Chrysostom does not use here—that it was the human nature of Christ that was ignorant, the explanation preferred by Gregory of Nazianzus: "We are to understand the ignorance in the most reverent sense, by attributing it to the manhood, not to the Godhead" (*Orat.* 4, 15). Apparently Chrysostom placed such significance on the intelligence of the Logos, that he avoided positing any kind of ignorance in Christ.

any other of his homilies or writings that would point to an active human intellect in the incarnate Son. Instead, intellect in Christ is always associated with his divine omniscience. On one gospel passage that describes Christ's anticipation of his disciples' opinion, Chrysostom comments "it is a proof of his divinity that he can bring to light unspoken thoughts."[173] Missing is any corresponding evidence of a human mind with limitations.

As in the case of the predominance of Christ's divinity over his occasional πάθος, here too Chrysostom sees no more than one active subject in all of Christ's earthly activities.[174]

## The Question of Two Wills

The question of the completeness of the human nature of Christ is in many ways the question of whether it could have opposed, or did oppose, Christ's divine nature. Volition is a central issue when the Greek Fathers consider the nature of God, for he is seen to extend his saving power to the world not out of necessity, but by the grace of the divine *oikonomia*. On the other hand, volition is key to understanding man's role in salvation according to those Fathers who incorporate moral participation in the act of salvation. As christological speculation deepened in the fourth century with various options being presented as to the singularity or plurality of natures in Christ, the issue of divine and human volition in the incarnate inevitably arose. In Chrysostom's time the question was hardly as specific as it eventually became in the post-Chalcedonain period when the monothelites continued to insist that a unified prosopon could possess only one will.

Some of Chrysostom's statements have been used as evidence for the doctrine of two wills in the decades before Chalcedon.[175]

---

[173] *Hom. in Jn.* 47, 2 (PG 59, 264).

[174] Cf. the same conclusion by Hay, "Integrity of the Human Nature," pp. 303-05.

[175] See Juzek, *Die Christologie*, p. 48. Chrysostom was used in support of the two wills doctrine by St. Maximus the Confessor and in the sixth ecumenical council in 681; see Hay, "Integrity of the Human Nature," p. 306.

Indeed, in two texts which we will shortly examine Chrysostom uses the phrase "two wills" in contexts where the Son's will seems to be distinguished from the Father's. A careful reading of the passages, however, must lead to the conclusion that Chrysostom did not understand Christ's humanity to embrace a distinct center of volition. The two most important occasions on which Chrysostom discusses the issue are both in polemical homilies, the seventh homily *On the Incomprehensible Nature of God* and in *In illud: Pater si possibile est*. Virtually all other discussions of the question arise in connection with gospel statements about the conformity of the Son's will to the Father's.

## Two Wills Opposed?

The seventh homily On the Incomprehensible Nature of God, a portion of which has already been discussed in a previous section, is one of the most important christological texts in the whole of Chrysostom. It contains one of his references to "two wills" quoted in later literature.

> So the heretics ask these questions: Is God afraid? Does he hesitate and shrink back? Does he feel pain?. . . . If they say that none of these feelings is worthy of God, then tell them that neither does Christ pray as God. Furthermore, if the words of Christ's prayer are the words of God, there is another absurdity involved. For the words not only reveal a struggle [ἀγωνίαν] but they point to two wills opposed to each other: one, the Son's, and the other, the Father's [ἀλλὰ καὶ δύο θελήματα, ἓν μὲν Ὑιοῦ, ἓν δὲ Πατρὸς, ἐναντία ἀλλήλοις]. Christ's words: "Not as I will but as you will" are the words of one who is making this clear. But those heretics never conceded this. When we constantly quote the text: "The Father and I are one" in connection with his power [ἐπὶ τῆς δυνάμεως], they keep saying that this was said in connection with the will [ἐπὶ τῆς θελήσεως] because they maintain that the will of the Father and of the Son is one [λέγοντες Πατρὸς καὶ Ὑιοῦ μίαν εἶναι βούλησιν]. However, if the will of the Father and the Son is one [εἰ τοίνυν Πατρὸς καὶ Ὑιοῦ μία βούλησίς ἐστι], how is it that Christ says in this text: "Yet not as I will but as you will? For if this statement had been made with a view to

his divinity [ἐπὶ τῆς θεότητος], there is a contradiction, and many absurdities arise from it. But if it was said in connection with his flesh [ἐπὶ τῆς σαρκὸς], the statement is reasonable, and there could be no grounds for blame or reproach.[176]

The line of thought leading up to this passage is an argument against any docetic interpretation of Christ. He was "conceived, born, and nurtured as any child would be," and even displays a human aversion to death—thus, the prayer in Gethsemane. The rhetorical question Chrysostom puts in the mouths of the heretics is supposed to show that they have left no distinction at all between divine essence and the incarnate experience of Christ. But Chrysostom wants to maintain a definite distinction. The scene represents a struggle arising from two opposing purposes: the necessities of the divine *oikonomia*, typified as the will of the Father, and the natural defenses of a real human life, typified as the will of the Son.

But whereas the full doctrine of two wills is the assertion of human and divine intent within the Son, the idea here is opposition between Father and Son, a related but different distinction.[177] The higher will pushing events ever closer to the Passion is not identified with the Logos within Christ, but the Father as distinguished from Christ. And the lower will resisting the agony is simply identified as that of the Son.[178] The defense, in other words, is more directed at trinitarian questions than christological,[179] and thus the comparison of the passage to the Chalcedonian understanding must be called into question.

---

[176] *De Incomprehensibili* 7, 6 (PG 48, 765f.). The continuation of this text is quoted above on p. 88 in connection with the reluctance of the flesh to undergo death.

[177] Perhaps opposition is even too strong for what Chrysostom means here. Ἐναντίος can mean "opposing," but more basically means "opposite" or "face to face."

[178] Chrysostom puts it simply: ἐν μὲν Υἱοῦ, ἐν δὲ Πατρὸς.

[179] The sermon is among the earliest preached by Chrysostom, and was specifically intended to address the lingering problems of the Arian controversy.

Yet the passage at least approaches some of the issues of the constitution of Christ's person. Two sets of parallel phrases, each used for the purpose of contrast, show that Chrysostom was aware that at least different modes of operation needed to be affirmed in the Son if he was genuinely human as well as divine. By using ἐπὶ τῆς δυνάμεως over against ἐπὶ τῆς θελήσεως—operation versus will—Chrysostom is saying that the unity of the Father and the Son consists in the power or authority proper to divinity, but not necessarily in will.[180] The second pair, ἐπὶ τῆς θεότητος and ἐπὶ τῆς σαρκὸς—divinity versus flesh—is more specifically a contrast of distinct modes of operation within the Son. Christ on a divine level only would not have had any hesitation with regard to the Father's will. To say anything else is to propose a "contradiction" and "absurdities." But because he possessed a real σάρξ the contrast of wills was not only possible, but even "reasonable."[181]

The way Chrysostom here distinguishes two different modes of operation in Christ minimizes the distinctness of two natures. It is certainly not a contrast of *logos* with *anthropos*. "Divinity" and "flesh" suffice for Chrysostom, two operations or activities of one subject called either "the Son" or simply "Christ." Also, when the contrary will is so closely identified with the flesh and its natural desire to preserve itself, the question arises just how high a human faculty this will is. If "flesh" is Chrysostom's word for human nature comprehensively considered, as Juzek maintains, then "will" may approximate full human volition; but if "flesh" is the equivalent of "body," then Hay is certainly right in questioning whether anything more than a physical principle of preservation is indicated here.

---

[180] Which is not to say that Chrysostom is here asserting that there are two wills within the Godhead. By "the Son" Chrysostom means Christ incarnate who, according to the gospels, shunned death.

[181] Note the previous discussion on the association of dread and agony with simple physical existence (pp. 85-93).

The second passage in which Chrysostom uses "two wills" is also used in a polemical homily and centers around the saying "not as I will, but as you will."

> For having said, "Let this cup pass from me" he added, "nevertheless not as I will but as you will." For herein as far as the actual expression is concerned [κατὰ τὴν ῥῆσιν] we find two wills opposed to one another [δύο θελήματα ἐναντία ἀλλήλοις], if at least the Father desires him to be crucified, but he himself does not desire it. And yet we everywhere behold him desiring and purposing the same things as the Father. For when he says "grant to them, as I and Thou are one that they also may be one in us," it is equivalent to saying that the purpose [γνώμην] of the Father and of the Son is one.[182]

Once again, Chrysostom does not hesitate to describe the Gethsemane scene as an opposition of wills, using the same phrase as he did in the seventh homily *On the Incomprehensible Nature of God*, δύο θελήματα ἐναντία ἀλλήλοις. He adds a slight qualification, however, in saying that it is opposition κατὰ τὴν ῥῆσιν. This is not to say that the opposition of wills is merely a linguistic peculiarity—Chrysostom takes the gospel accounts more literally than that. There really was a point of divergence of wills, but that does not have to imply an essential independence or separation between the will of the Father and the will of the Son. "Not as I will but as you will," in other words, ought not to be taken as a general description of relations between the Father and the Son. That is borne out, says Chrysostom, by all the expressions of unity between the Father and the Son which is the ordinary state of their relationship. Why then the divergence here? Chrysostom goes on to explain the importance of the reality of the flesh of Christ against Marcion, Valentinus, the Manichees, and "many more heretics."[183] The reality of his flesh is evidenced by a

---

[182] *In illud: Pater si possibile est* 3 (PG 51, 36).

[183] We may find evidence for understanding how much or how little Chrysostom is including in the expression "the flesh" of Christ by identifying the heretical tendencies he is addressing here. If lingering docetism is the concern, "flesh" does not have to mean more than body; but if the Arians are in view, then

real birth, real growth, and eventually real suffering which itself is displayed most graphically in the conflict of wills in the garden. There was actual opposition because the Son was actually human.

As in the passage from *On the Incomprehensible Nature of God* previously considered Chrysostom is here making a distinction between the Father and the Son, not between two centers of consciousness within Christ. But also here again conflict is a possibility because Christ is capable of two different modes of operation. The terminology suggests a single acting subject, but the concept allows for two very different kinds of activities.

## Unity of Will

The Gethsemane passage provided the Fathers with a locus classicus for discussions of wills in Christ, if for no other reason than that opponents of orthodoxy made frequent use of it. One wonders what course the christological discussions of the fourth and fifth centuries would have taken if that one unique saying, "not my will," did not appear in the gospels.

Nevertheless, other biblical texts raise the same issues, and Chrysostom is eager to reconcile the apparent difficulties as he reaches such passages. It is especially in the homilies on John that Chrysostom encounters other expressions of the distinction of wills which necessitate comment. Unlike the Gethsemane pericope, however, these passages contain no direct statement of the opposition of wills, only their comparison. For instance, Christ's statement: "I seek not my own will, but the will of him who sent me,"[184] is implicitly problematic for Chrysostom. There is no anguish or suffering here to attract the attention of Christ's will away from the divine plan, only the open-ended opportunity for the Son to demonstrate the perfect will of the Father. Chrysostom responds, as if addressing Christ:

---

Chrysostom may be speaking to their soulless understanding of Christ's humanity and "flesh" would then have a much fuller meaning.

[184] Jn. 5:30.

What is it you are saying? Do you have a will other than the Father's [θέλημα ἕτερον παρὰ τὸν Πατέρα]? Yet, elsewhere you have said: "Even as you and I are one." And again, speaking with regard to harmony of will [ἐπὶ θελήματος λέγων καὶ ὁμονοίας].

Chrysostom quotes several biblical texts that indicate unity of will between the Father and the Son, then continues the explanation:

What he implied is some such truth as this: not that the Father wills one thing and he another [ἄλλο . . . ἄλλο],[185] but, "just as an individual soul has one will, so my will and the Father's are one [ὥσπερ μιᾶς διανοίας ἓν θέλημα, οὕτως ἐμοῦ καὶ τοῦ Πατρός]. Now, do not wonder if he has spoken of so close a union [συνάφειαν].

Chrysostom illustrates this principle by 1 Cor. 2:11 which he takes as descriptive of the closeness of union between the Spirit and the Father,[186] then continues:

Christ was saying nothing else than this: "I will nothing exclusively, apart from the Father [ἕτερον καὶ ἴδιον παρὰ Πατρὸς]," but if he wills anything, this I also will; and if I will anything, this he also wills . . . The decision of each of us proceeds from the same opinion [γνώμης]. If he discoursed on these matters in a somewhat human fashion, do not be surprised. . . . notice that he said: "I seek not my own will." Is his will, then different from and also very inferior [to the Father's]; nay, not merely inferior but even ineffectual? Because, if it was capable of effecting salvation and conformed [συμβαῖνον] to that of the Father why did you not seek it? Men, indeed, might rightly speak in this fashion, since they have many desires contrary to what God wills, but why do you say this, if you are like the Father in all respects?[187]

---

185 Elsewhere: "Is your will one thing and his [the Father's] another [ἕτερον... ἕτερον]?" (*Hom. in Jn.* 45, 3 [PG 59, 254]).

186 "For what person knows a man's thoughts except the spirit of the man which is in him? So no one comprehends the thoughts of God except the Spirit of God."

187 *Hom. in Jn.* 39, 4 (PG 59, 226).

Chrysostom's somewhat forced explanation finally is that Christ was showing humility by defending himself in "human language," that is, by taking the stance of one whose unity with God the Father could not necessarily be assumed. The reality, however, is that Christ's will was one with the Father's.

Chrysostom strongly affirms the union by using συνάφεια, one of the key terms in the christological controversy. Συνάφεια or conjunction, is, for Theodore of Mopsuestia as well as for Nestorius, an appropriate way of describing the unity of the one *prosopon* of Christ that still maintains the integrity of the two natures.[188] Cyril, however, is unsatisfied with its use because he does not think it expresses the union adequately.[189] The two natures of Christ are related to each other in ἔνωσις, an essential unity. The same term was used by Apollinaris as well, and so it is not surprising that it suggested to many, including Nestorius, a union of hypostases into one φύσις. Though συνάφεια eventually became a test word for heterodoxy, Chrysostom can be numbered among those writers who use the word less technically before the days of Nestorius.[190]

The anthropological analogy of the conjunction of mind with will further emphasizes the closeness of unity Chrysostom is suggesting existed between the will of the Father and that of Christ. Apollinaris had defended a complete ἔνωσις of human and divine by comparing the constitution of the Christ with that of ordinary human beings whom he saw as unified persons

---

[188] Nestorius speaks of "the distinction of natures in accordance with the special characteristics of humanity and deity, the conjunction of these natures in one person." (Nestorius' Second Letter to Cyril, trans. in Norris, *The Christological Controversy*, p. 137).

[189] "We do not worship a human being in conjunction with the Logos, lest the appearance of a division creep in by reason of that phrase 'in conjunction with.'" (Cyril's Second Letter to Nestorius, trans. in Norris, *The Christological Controversy*, p. 134).

[190] See, for example, Basil, *ep.* 210, 5 (PG 32, 776) and Gregory of Nyssa, C. *Eun.* 5 (PG 45, 705). Συνάφεια also occurs in a key christological statement by Chrysostom, *Hom. in Jn.* 11, 2 (PG 59, 80), to be treated in a later section.

responding with two inner faculties, the higher rational soul and the lower animal soul. But whereas Apollinaris was describing the essential existences of comparable beings, Chrysostom was only using an analogy. Otherwise the logical consequence of his comparison is the blurring of distinctions between the Father and the Son, something Chrysostom is always careful to avoid.

Thus, Chrysostom argues for a unity of will between the Father and the Son. And since by "Christ," Chrysostom means "Christ incarnate with all of the human characteristics he bore in the economy," he is saying that there is no real distinction of wills within the person of Christ.

Chrysostom describes a kind of sovereignty of will in Christ with regard to the Passion. Christ was never actually compelled to do anything or go anywhere, not when threatened by a menacing crowd or a hostile city,[191] and certainly not in his arrest and crucifixion. The fact that Jesus gave up his spirit "knowing that all was now finished,"[192] showed that:

> . . . every detail was controlled by the one who was dying, and death did not enter his body until he himself willed it, and he willed it only after all had been fulfilled. That is why he had said: "I have power to lay down my life and I have power to take it up again."[193]

The same is evidenced by his coming to Jerusalem, going out to the garden, even allowing himself to be kissed by Judas. Chrysostom sees the divine will as determining every action of Christ—he acts, but is never the passive object of the actions of another.

---

[191] Commenting on Christ's retreat at the news of John the Baptist's death, Chrysostom says: "For it is his will ordinarily to conduct things after the manner of a man (τὰ γὰρ πλείονα ἀνθρωπινώτερον βούλεται διοικεῖν), the time not yet calling him to reveal his Godhead plainly." There is one will controlling both the manifestations of humanity and divinity. *Hom. in Matt.* 49, 1 (PG 58, 495).

[192] John 19:28.

[193] *Hom. in Jn.* 85, 2 (PG 59, 462).

But the picture becomes more complicated by Chrysostom's use of Christ's willingness to die as an example for human obedience. Chrysostom states:

> In addition to this, he wished also to establish the point that it was not unwillingly that he went to his death (for, if it were against his will, how would the deed evoke the Father's love?) and also that his was very much in conformity with the Father's will."[194]

And elsewhere:

> It was to teach us this lesson by his example that Christ went to his passion, not by compulsion or by necessity, but willingly. . . . He was showing his disciples that he was going to his passion willingly, for this fact was sufficient to give them very great courage.[195]

This would seem to imply a human act of willing, for how could the act be meritorious and exemplary if not rooted in a freely acting human nature? Evidently the question did not occur to Chrysostom because he does not attempt to harmonize the sovereign nature of the will of Christ on the one hand with its exemplary nature on the other. Once again, Chrysostom simply attributes to one acting subject motives and operations that other writers from Antioch would distinguish into distinct natures or hypostases.

To summarize:

1. Though he deals with the idea of two wills only when the biblical text requires explanation, Chrysostom nevertheless affirms an identifiable human will in the incarnate Christ.

2. Because it is a consequence of the event of the incarnation and evidence of its reality, the human will does have theological significance, although that significance is limited by the range of experience Chrysostom attributes to that will. Because he links the

---

[194] *Hom. in Jn.* 60, 2 (PG 59, 330).

[195] *Hom. in Jn.* 83, 1 (PG 59, 447).

human volition of Christ only with the self-preserving nature of the human σάρξ[196] (at least when there is a conflict of wills) he is certainly stopping short of postulating a fully-functioning human will in Christ. Thus the human will is an identification of Christ with the race on the level of body, but not necessarily soul.

3. Though a distinction of wills may be spoken of, it is only because the gospel accounts of the Passion attest to it, not because it is an ontological necessity for salvation. The conflict of wills is a unique event precipitated only by the most catastrophic threat to the fleshly humanity of Christ.

4. The ordinary expression is one of complete unity of wills between the Father and the incarnate Son. Chrysostom sees the divine principle as so predominating over the human, that any degree of divergence of intent is unthinkable. Jesus' statements about his conformity to the Father's will are virtually tautological. They are expressions of fact with no conditionality whatsoever, stated in the way they are in order to encourage obedience in disciples.

5. Thus in an unusual sense, Christ is an exemplar of human obedience, but not because he actually accomplished obedience on a human level. Christ's life is a picture of, but not an experiment in, conformity of will with God. The question of moral obedience and its salvific importance will be treated more fully in a later section, but it may be noted at this point that these texts on the volitional activity of Jesus associate Chrysostom with the so-called "Antiochene" school only superficially.

## Human Nature as "Flesh"

The operations of emotion, intellect, and will are important anthropological categories against which the Christology of the Fathers may be tested, as was just done in the case of Chrysostom. But, of course, affirmations of the human nature of Christ may come up independently of any such functional

---

[196] Cf. Hay, "Integrity of the Human Nature," p. 309.

descriptions, and it is to some of the important texts in this category that we now turn. Reserved for the following chapter are those texts which describe the relationship of the divine and the human in Christ.

Throughout the homilies and writings of Chrysostom there is one favorite expression for the humanity of Christ: flesh. What needs to be determined is just what the content of this σάρξ is, that is, whether it may include characteristics beyond those of the body even including those of the rational soul. There are a few instances in which Chrysostom explicitly uses the term for "soul" and those will have to be examined in due course, but given the far more frequent use of σάρξ, it is first necessary to understand its meaning. The point is significant, for traditional treatments of Chrysostom understand the doctrine of two natures to be adequately accounted for in Chrysostom on the basis that he uses σάρξ as inclusive of body and soul. Such is the argument of Juzek.[197] Hay, to the contrary, thinks Chrysostom does not envision Christ's humanity as consisting of anything more than real corporeality. Whatever the case, the solution will not be found simply in the terminology used. As Maurice Wiles indicates, the word "flesh" was used by writers (e.g. Tertullian) who clearly affirm a human soul in Christ, and, conversely, the term "man" does not necessarily imply a rational soul.[198]

---

[197] "Wenn Chrysostomus von der Gottheit und Menschheit in ihrer Verbindung spricht, so gebraucht er das Wort "σάρξ," nie "ἄνθρωπος," um nicht eine Verwirrung zu schaffen, weil ἄνθρωπος bei ihm eine vollkommene menschliche Person bezeichnet. Und wenn nun der Sohn Gottes hinzutritt, so würde es ja in der Tat zwei Personen in Christus geben: eine rein menschliche und eine rein göttliche. Indem er also von σάρξ spricht, die er, wie wir gesehen, als vollständige Menschheit, d. h. als Verbindung von Leib und Seele aufgefaßt wissen will, geht er obiger Schwierigkeit aus dem Wege. Nur bei der Erhöhung der menschlichen Natur Christi nach der Auferstehung gebraucht er das Wort ἄνθρωπος statt σάρξ—ein Wort, das dann Fakundus von Hermiane sich zunutze machte, indem er es im Sinne des Theodor von Mopsuestia deutete, d. h. als Beweis für die Zweipersonenlehre" (Juzek, *Die Christologie*, pp. 34f.).

[198] Maurice Wiles, "The Nature of the Early Debate about Christ's Soul," *J Eccl H* 16 (1965): 140.

## Anthropological Assumptions

Σάρξ is a term of some ambiguity within the New Testament. "Flesh" in classical usage included the corruptible aspect of humanity over against the incorruptibility which was a natural characteristic of ψυχή. In a further development, Epicurus saw the flesh as the seat of human emotion and passion because of its susceptibility to stimuli.[199] The use of "flesh" in the New Testament is found predominantly in the Pauline literature where it sometimes simply designates the body,[200] but elsewhere includes that aspect of humanity which stands in need of redemption and is in some sense the source of sin.[201]

Paul's juxtaposition of good and evil inclinations in the human personality comes out most clearly perhaps in Rom. 6 and 7. In clarifying such statements as "It is no longer I that do it, but sin which dwells within me; for I know that nothing good dwells within me, that is, in my flesh," Chrysostom finds it necessary to refute the notion that flesh is essentially evil, an idea prevalent in the Greek world and still a problem in the church of the late fourth century. (Chrysostom finds Paul at this point "not very clear.") Here are revealed some of Chrysostom's anthropological assumptions which will be instructive in understanding his view of Christ's humanity.

> For the fact that "no good thing dwelleth in it," does not show that it is evil itself. Now we admit, that the flesh is not so great as the soul, and is inferior to it, yet not contrary, or opposed to it, or evil; but, that it is beneath the soul, as a harp beneath a harper, and as a ship under the pilot. And these are not contrary to those who guide and use them, but go with them entirely. . . . And this Paul here points out, giving the governing

---

[199] *Theological Dictionary of the New Testament*, ed. G. Kittel and G. Friedrich, 7:100-151, s. v. "σάρξ," by E. Schweizer.

[200] E. g. 1 Cor. 5:5; 2 Cor. 12:7; Gal. 4:13.

[201] E. g. Gal. 5:17-21 "For the desires of the flesh are against the Spirit, and the desires of the Spirit are against the flesh; for these are opposed to each other. . . .the works of the flesh are plain: fornication, impurity, licentiousness. . . ."

> power to the soul, and after dividing man into these two things,
> the soul and the body, he says, that the flesh has less of
> reason, and is destitute of discretion, and ranks among things to
> be led, not among things that lead. But the soul has more
> wisdom, and can see what is to be done and what not, yet is not
> equal to pulling in the horse as it wishes. And this would be a
> charge not against the flesh only, but against the soul also,
> which knows indeed what it ought to do, but still does not carry
> out in practice what seems best to it. . . . Do you see how he
> acquits the essence of the soul, as well as the essence of the
> flesh from accusation, and removes it entirely to sinful
> actions?[202]

The argument that follows is that sin is the outcome of acts of the
will made in the tension between good and wicked possibilities.
Although Chrysostom provides no specific explanation regarding
the genesis of evil choices, he is certain it is not to be traced to an
essential wickedness of either the flesh or the soul. The flesh is
"weak" and thus essentially passive, possessing no impetus to act
on its own. Paul's phrase "carnally minded" raises problems, for
it seems to ascribe acts of rationality to the body, but Chrysostom
explains: "He does not speak of the nature of the flesh, or the
essence of the body, but of being carnally 'minded'. . . . And in
saying thus, he does not ascribe to the flesh any reasoning power
of its own."[203] Here σάρξ equals σῶμα and it is divorced from any
of the characteristics of ψυχή. Whether or not the same holds true
in christological discussions remains to be seen.

The discussion of Rom. 7 leads naturally to the question of the
flesh of Christ in which Chrysostom finds evidence for the
essential goodness of flesh.

> So you see it is sin that gets condemned everywhere, and not the
> flesh, for this is crowned with honor. . . . But if he does say that
> it was "in the likeness" of flesh that he sent the Son, do not
> therefore suppose that his flesh was of a different kind. For as
> he called it "sinful," this was why he put the word "likeness."

---

[202] *Hom. in Rom.* 13 (Field 1, 101).

[203] *Hom. in Rom.* 13 (Field 1, 104-05).

For sinful flesh it was not that Christ had, but like indeed to our sinful flesh, yet sinless, and in nature the same with us. And so even from this it is plain that by nature the flesh was not evil.[204]

Thus consubstantiality with regard to flesh is affirmed, and that for soteriological reasons. This was "the method of the victory," that "He took no other flesh, but this very one which was beset with troubles." And what makes this means of salvation "the greatest possible marvel" is that Christ's victory consisted in "the flesh not being conquered by sin, its even conquering and condemning it, [and] its not condemning it barely, but condemning it as having sinned."[205] While the reality of the flesh is crucial, Chrysostom makes no mention of consubstantiality between Christ and the human race with specific regard to the soul. Chrysostom has so clearly identified the soul as the active, determinative faculty of humanity—that which has "reason" and "wisdom," the harper instead of the harp—that he gravitates toward the more passive aspect, the flesh, when speaking of the human nature of Christ.

That "flesh" is a summary term for Chrysostom when speaking of human nature—be it our nature fraught with need or his, complete and unspoiled—is further brought out by the frequency with which the two are verbally parallel. Christ was formed from the flesh of a woman "that no one might think that the child was of another nature than ours."[206] His taking on flesh shows that he "took not on him an angel's nature, but man's."[207] There is nothing to indicate in any of Chrysostom's homilies that

---

[204] *Hom. in Rom.* 13 (Field 1, 105).

[205] *Hom. in Rom.* 13 (Field 1, 104-05).

[206] *Hom. in Jn.* 26, 1 (PG 59, 154). That Christ's human nature is fully derived from the flesh he received through the Virgin is also stated in *Hom. in Matt.* 12, 1 (PG 57, 201): Christ "vouchsafed to be borne. . . in a virgin's womb and to come forth thence with our nature"; in *Hom. in Matt.* 44, 3 (PG 57, 467): "He came to us by being clothed with flesh," and elsewhere.

[207] *Hom. in Heb.* 5, 1 (PG 63, 45).

by "human nature" he means anything more than that which is predicated of "flesh." And the only difference between Christ's flesh and ours is that his is untainted by sin—and even there the difference is not immense because even our flesh, disappointing though it may be, is not essentially sinful.[208]

### Clothing and Temple Imagery

Chrysostom likes to use the familiar "clothing" metaphor when describing the fleshly nature of Christ. Ἐνδύω is one of those words in the early Christian world that was useful for the heterodox who wanted to minimize or eliminate the real humanity of Christ, and favored by orthodox writers who simply liked the metaphor. So, for example, Ebionites, Gnostics and Docetists were criticized for their understanding of the "clothing," but Clement of Alexandria uses it in a non-controversial way to describe the incarnation.[209] It occurs frequently in another Alexandrian, Athanasius, when speaking of the event and the result of the incarnation.[210] Because he evidently did not stress Christ's human nature containing a rational soul,[211] the clothing metaphor was perfectly adequate for Athanasius.

Chrysostom finds in the clothing metaphor not just a description of the incarnation but of the human condition in general. Christ ministered to "men encompassed with flesh and

---

[208] This closeness of identity between Christ and ordinary human beings is still, of course, only from the perspective of Christ considered humanly. The gap becomes infinite when the discussion concerns Christ's "pure nature" (see Chap. 4).

[209] "Him. . . who for us clothed himself with humanity" (*Stromateis* 4, 21). Note Clement's typological understanding of the high priest's robe as Christ's "ministry in the flesh," which he put on (ἐνδύω) when he descended into the region of sense (*Stromateis* 5, 7).

[210] E.g. "for this reason the Savior rightly put on (ἐνεδύσατο) a body in order that the body, being joined to life, might no longer remain as mortal in death, but having put on (ἐνδυσάμενον) immortality, might then rise up and remain immortal" (*De incarnatione* 44, 6).

[211] See Grillmeier, *Christ in Christian Tradition*, pp. 308-28.

subject to the necessities of nature."[212] The great human excuse for sin is "I am entangled with a body, I am clothed with flesh, I dwell in the world, I abide on earth," to which the proper response is that Christ too "was encompassed with flesh."[213] Thus flesh implies weakness and need, but not inevitable depravity. Nevertheless, it is where sin takes hold—the substance it uses (not purely in a material sense, of course)—and thus the realm of human existence that God takes and transforms.[214] By being encompassed in flesh, Christ identified himself with the human race at the most ordinary level. He can even call other human beings brethren (Heb. 2:12) because "when he clothed himself with flesh, he clothed himself also with the brotherhood, and at the same time came in the brotherhood."[215] Chrysostom thus uses clothing imagery to reinforce the reality of the assumption of human flesh by Christ. It is by no means the strongest way of describing the fullness of humanity in the incarnate, but it is certainly not employed in order to minimize it.

Closely related to the concept of clothing is another metaphor that was bound to become controversial as the human nature of Christ became the subject for further speculation in the fourth and fifth centuries: the humanity as a temple ($\nu\alpha\acuteos$). It is by Antiochenes like Theodore of Mopsuestia and Nestorius that the metaphor is used as a way of keeping the human nature distinct from the divine nature.[216] Rowan Greer points out that "temple" is

---

[212] ἀνθρώποις... σάρκα περικειμένοις, καὶ ἀνάγκῃ φύσεως ὑποκειμένοις (Hom. in Matt. 19, 5 [PG 57, 280]).

[213] *Hom. in Matt.* 43, 3 (PG 57, 455).

[214] Chrysostom expresses this taking of flesh in the incarnation in quite vivid terms. In response to Heb. 2:14 "he [Christ] likewise partook of the same nature," he says: "it is derived from the figure of persons pursuing those who turn away from them.... For when human nature was fleeing from him... he pursued after and overtook us" (*Hom. in Heb.* 5, 1 [PG 63, 46]).

[215] *Hom. in Heb.* 4, 3 (PG 63, 41).

[216] E.g. in Nestorius' second letter to Cyril: "He is entirely the son of David according to the flesh but Lord according to the deity. The body therefore is the

a frequently-used biblical metaphor and so typifies Theodore as
an exegete and theologian more motivated by biblical categories
than the neo-Platonic ontological concepts employed by the
Alexandrians.[217] There is no doubting the biblical background of
the image,[218] but it is also true that it becomes more heavily used
by writers wanting to emphasize the distinctness of the humanity
of Christ. Whether Chrysostom used the term for this purpose or,
like Athanasius and others, for its vividness and as a way of
describing the uniqueness of Christ's being, may be seen by the
contexts of the passages in which it occurs. The infancy is one
obvious place for Chrysostom to speak of the Lord's "temple":

> How, I pray thee, did the Spirit frame [ἔπλασεν] that Temple?
> How did he take not all the flesh from the womb, but a part
> thereof, and increased it and fashioned it [ηὔξησε καὶ
> διετύπωσεν]? For that he did come forth of the Virgin's flesh,
> he hath declared by speaking of "that which was conceived in
> her," and Paul, by saying, "made of a woman" whereby he stops
> the mouths of them that say, Christ came among us as through
> some channel [διά τινος σωλῆνος]. For, if this were so, what
> need of the womb? If this were so, he hath nothing in common
> with us, but that flesh is of some other kind, and not of the mass
> which belongs to us [οὐ τοῦ φυράματος τοῦ ἡμετέρου]. . . .
> Therefore that he was of us [ἐξ ἡμῶν], and of our substance [τοῦ
> φυράματος τοῦ ἡμετέρου], and of the virgin's womb, is manifest
> from these things, and from others beside; but how, is not also
> manifest.[219]

---

temple of the Son's deity, and a temple united to it by a complete and divine
conjunction," trans. in Norris, *The Christological Controversy*, p. 138.

[217] R. A. Greer, *Theodore of Mopsuestia: Exegete and Theologian* (London,
1961). With regard to indwelling and temple language Greer says: "Nowhere in
Theodore does his rejection of Alexandrian, Platonic modes of thought appear
more clearly. . . Theodore is striving to express the union in as careful and
philosophic a way as possible. Yet throughout his terms are Biblical and ethical
in their import" (p. 57).

[218] Most importantly, Jn. 2:19: "Destroy this temple and in three days I will
raise it up."

[219] *Hom. in Matt.* 4, 3 (PG 57, 43).

Clearly Chrysostom considers the material nature of the incarnate Son and its origin a major aspect of the mystery of the economy. That divinity formed a unique vessel for its habitation is established tradition—how the immaterial principle could so closely utilize the material is "what is kept secret." Gnostic theories that keep spirit and matter separate, viewing Mary as a channel[220] instead of a source of the incarnate Son, miss the very point of the incarnation—identification in substance. This term φύραμα, "mass, bulk," is used figuratively in Rom. 9:21 for the unformed substance—the lump of clay—out of which God fashions various kinds of human vessels, and the Fathers continue to use it as a metaphor for human substance.[221] Thus Chrysostom portrays the fleshly nature of Christ in vivid terms, but does not move beyond the material identification. There is no hint that what lies behind his choice of "temple" is a strong differentiation between the humanity of the Lord and his divinity. It is rather a manner of speaking that takes the sting out of any docetic accusation that bodily incarnation is inappropriate and impossible for deity.[222]

Chrysostom uses a related image—a tabernacle—in much the same way. It is Jn. 1:14 "And the Word was made flesh and dwelt

---

[220] Irenaeus rejects this image of Christ as "he who passed through Mary as water goes through a channel," the Valentinian understanding of the incarnation. *Adv. haer.* 1, 7, 2.

[221] Basil, *ep.* 262, 1; Gregory of Nazianzus, *Orat.* 14, 15; and Gregory of Nyssa, *hom. in 1 Cor.* 15:28. That Chrysostom uses φύραμα here instead of οὐσία or some other common ontological term should not be taken to mean that Chrysostom was avoiding the ontological identification.

[222] Chrysostom uses ναός in a similar way in another homily on Matthew when explaining how the Son of God should be an infant who must flee as any mortal: "Neither is a temple framed at once, but a regular conception takes place, and a time of nine months, and pangs, and a delivery, and giving suck, and silence for so long a space, and he awaits the age proper to manhood that by all means acceptance might be won for the mystery of the economy" (*Hom. in Matt.* 8, 3 [PG 57, 86]).

(tabernacled, ἐσκήνωσεν) among us" that prompts him to comment on the manner of and reason for the "dwelling."[223]

> What, then, is the dwelling [σκηνή] where he dwelt? Listen to the Prophet saying: "I will raise up the tabernacle of David that has fallen [Amos 9:11]." Actually, it has fallen, our nature has had an irreparable fall, and was in need of that powerful hand alone. For it was not possible to raise it up otherwise, unless he who fashioned it in the beginning stretched out a hand to it and formed it again [διατυπώσαντος][224] from above by the regeneration of water and the Spirit. . . . He dwells always in this tabernacle, for he put on our flesh, not to put it off again, but to have it always with him. If this were not so, he would not have deemed it worthy of his royal throne and, bearing it [with him], would not have had it adored by all the host above.[225]

It would be a mistake to attribute to Chrysostom any intention of holding the human nature of Christ as quite distinct from the divine in using such language of indwelling. The expressions arise from the biblical text itself, and if Chrysostom emphasizes anything it is the merging of the divine Word with human flesh. In fact, the union is permanent—humanity has entered heaven because Christ's real flesh has. In many homilies Chrysostom reaffirms that the ascension of Christ with human flesh results in human nature itself being carried into heaven. In this way the passive role of humanity and the active grace of God is emphasized—God "stretched out a hand," or, as Chrysostom puts it elsewhere: "human nature did not go up to heaven, but he himself came to it, rightly despised and worthless as it was, and when the espousals had taken place he did not permit it to remain longer here, but took it away and brought it to his Father's

---

[223] Chrysostom does not ignore the difficulties raised by Christ being made flesh (see Chap. 4).

[224] Used elsewhere by Chrysostom for natural human generation, e.g.: *Hom. in Matt.* 4, 3 (PG 57, 43).

[225] *Hom. in Jn.* 11, 2 (PG 59, 80).

house."[226] One of the ways the Word-flesh Christology is often distinguished from the Word-man is by its conception of the humanity of Christ in an abstract rather than concrete sense. This statement of Chrysostom's is evidence that he interpreted the flesh or dwelling of Christ to be broader than the concrete life of an individual man. When the Logos took flesh he took the fallen nature of the entire race and refashioned it.

### Development in the God-Man

One final point may be made about human nature as "flesh" in Chrysostom. Any time the issue of development in Christ comes up, Chrysostom seems to express it in a more or less physical way. Lk. 2:52 "And Jesus increased in wisdom and in stature, and in favor with God and man" was a weapon in the arsenal of Arians who reasoned that development meant change and since divinity is by nature immutable, Christ could not have been divine. The response made to the Arians was either to admit real psychological and physical development but to attribute it to a quite distinct human nature, as did the Antiochenes, or to minimize the psychological aspect of Christ's development, thus leaving Lk. 2:52 as a simple description of physical growth, as did the Alexandrians. Chrysostom's own approach is more akin to the latter.[227]

To summarize, then, why flesh is Chrysostom's preferred way of speaking about Christ's humanity, we may first note that

---

[226] *Hom. in Jn.* 18, 2 (PG 59, 115). Also: "our nature has been carried up into Heaven" (*Hom. in Matt.* 1, 1 [PG 57, 15]); and "it is a great and wonderful thing... that our flesh should sit on high, and be adored by Angels.... God has great zeal on behalf of our nature" (*Hom. in Heb.* 5, 1 [PG 63, 46-47]).

[227] He nowhere directly explains Lk. 2:52, but whenever he speaks of the growing Christ, it is in connection with defending the reality of the flesh. So, for example, in commenting on "it behooved [him] in all things to be made like his brethren" (Heb. 2:17) Chrysostom says: "What is this, 'in all things'? He was born (he means), was brought up, grew, suffered all things necessary, and at last he died" *Hom. in Heb.* 5, 1 (PG 63, 47).

"flesh" was a well-established way of expressing the reality of the incarnation from the second century up into the fourth and fifth centuries, not necessarily disregarding the soul. Athanasius and others were not campaigning against the idea of a real human soul in Christ as much as they were understanding the passive aspect of man—and the philosophical milieu of the day understood the flesh to be that aspect—as the battleground where sin frequently gains the upper hand and where the redemptive renewal must take place. Far from a simple spirit-flesh dualism, this theory regards God as having sovereignly overwhelmed humanity by assuming it in the dimension where it has experienced its own suffering the most. As Frances Young points out,[228] if a human νοῦς or ψυχή in Christ seems neglected in this scheme it is because it is not really necessary. While this may sound Apollinarian, it is not, for Athanasius, Cyril, and others usually identified with the Word-flesh type Christology knew that a real soul had to be posited of Christ, but a soul more benign, more impressionable. Such Alexandrians did not feel compelled, as did Antiochenes like Theodore of Mopsuestia and Nestorius, to view Christ as the divine Son conjoined to a freely operating human who accomplished salvation by actively fulfilling the requirements of righteous living. It would seem only logical that the former monk and sometimes highly moralistic preacher of Antioch and Constantinople would naturally reflect the more active view of salvation rather than the passive, but his most common christological assumptions involve a humanity or "flesh" of Christ that remains always the passive instrument of the Logos.

## *Did Christ Have a Human Soul?*

The overwhelming use of "flesh" as the designation for the humanity of Christ becomes even more apparent when one starts looking for specific affirmations of a human soul. We have already seen in Chrysostom's exegesis of Rom. 7 a common

---

[228] Frances Young, "A Reconsideration of Alexandrian Christology," *J Eccl H* 22 (1971): 103-14.

anthropological scheme where the soul, being the seat of reason and wisdom, is essentially the governing power over the passive flesh.[229]

Maurice Wiles explains that though a human soul in Christ is clearly affirmed as early as Tertullian and Origen (though for different reasons—Tertullian's being soteriological and Origen's mediatorial) it is recognized as problematic for the unity of Christ by the fourth century. Though something of an embarrassment, the Fathers recognized that "Scripture did speak in such terms, and, therefore, the idea was allowed to drop tacitly out of use rather than be directly and explicitly denied."[230]

The single most important passage on the human soul of Christ occurs in Chrysostom's seventh homily on Philippians. That this homily[231] should be christologically important is not surprising since it is based upon one of the most important christological passages of the New Testament, the hymn in Philippians. Here Chrysostom has the opportunity to explain to his Constantinopolitan audience[232] how Christ existed in the "form" (μορφή) of God, but then was somehow "emptied" and made "in the likeness of men." Elucidation of these simple phrases dominates both the sixth and the seventh homilies in the series for they were closely linked with the condemned theories of

---

[229] See *Theological Dictionary of the New Testament*, ed. G. Kittel and G. Friedrich, 9:608-60, s. v. "Ψυχή," by K. Tröger.

[230] Maurice Wiles, "The Nature of the Early Debate about Christ's Soul," *J Eccl H* 16 (1965): 144.

[231] This homily will also require comment with regard to the relationship of the two natures in a subsequent chapter.

[232] Hay ("Integrity of the Human Nature," p. 301) identifies representatives for and against a Constantinople dating. For: B. de Montfaucon, "Monitum ad Homilias in Epistolam ad Philippenses," PG 62, 177f.; H. Lietzmann, "Johannes Chrysostomus," in *Pauly-Wissowa Realencyclopädie*, 18e: 1819; W. Stoderl, *Kommentar zu den Briefen des hl. Paulus an die Philipper und Kolosser* in *Bibliothek der Kirchenväter*, (München, 1924), pp. 1-4; and especially M. von Bonsdorff, *Zur Predigttätigkeit des Joh. Chrysostomus* (Helsinki, 1922), pp. 78-82. Against (in favor of Antioch): J. Stilting, *Acta Sanctorum*. Sept. IV, p.4 64; and C. Baur, *John Chrysostom*, vol. 2, p. 62.

not one or two heretics, but the longest list Chrysostom gives anywhere.[233] The contested point, of course, is whether or not such expressions as μορφῇ θεοῦ, μορφὴν δούλου, and ἐν ὁμοιώματι ἀνθρώπων γενόμενος imply that either the divinity or the humanity was something less than real. Not surprisingly, Chrysostom vehemently rejects either interpretation, and that becomes the occasion for an explict reference to a soul in Christ.

> What then means, "Being made in the likeness of men"? He had many things belonging to us, and many he had not; for instance, he was not born of wedlock. He did no sin. These things had he which no man has. He was not what he seemed only [τὸ φαινόμενον μόνον], but he was God also; he seemed to be a man, but he was not like the mass of men. For he was like them in flesh. He means then, that he was not a mere man. On account of this he says, "in the likeness of men." *For we indeed are soul and body, but he was God, and soul and body* [ἡμεῖς μὲν γὰρ ψυχὴ καὶ σῶμά ἐσμεν· ἐκεῖνος δὲ θεὸς, καὶ ψυχὴ, καὶ σῶμα]. On account of this, he says, "in the likeness." For lest when you hear that he emptied himself [ἐκένωσεν ἑαυτὸν], you should think that some change [μεταβολὴν], and degeneracy [μετάπτωσιν], and loss [ἀφανισμόν] is here; *he says, while he remained what he was, he took that which he was not, and being made flesh he remained God, in that he was the Word* [μένων, φησὶν, ὃ ἦν, ἔλαβεν ὃ οὐκ ἦν, καὶ σὰρξ γενόμενος ἔμενε θεὸς λόγος ὤν]. In this then he was like man, and for this cause Paul says, "and in fashion [σχήματι]." Not that his nature degenerated [μετέπεσεν], nor that any confusion [σύγχυσις] arose, but he became man in fashion.... Paul did not say that he had not flesh, but that that flesh sinned not, but was like sinful flesh. Like in what? *In nature, not in sin; therefore his was like a sinful soul* [διὰ τοῦτο ὁμοία ἁμαρτωλοῦ ψυχῆς].[234]

This text represents the most direct affirmation Chrysostom makes of a human soul in Christ. It is clear and straightforward,

---

[233] This theological gallery of rogues includes Arius, Paul of Samosata, Marcellus, Sabellius, Marcion, Valentinus, Manes, Photinus, Sophronius and Apollinaris. The errors of each are treated in kind. *Hom. in Phil.* 7 (Field 5, 31).

[234] (Italics added.) *Hom. in Phil.* 8 (Field 5, 40).

almost in equation form. The last, somewhat puzzling phrase seems intended not to lessen the reality of the soul, but to further explain that Paul uses "likeness" to distinguish Christ's soul from ordinary souls because his was sinless. There is nothing, however, that would indicate what kind of soul, and what its functions may be. There are two erroneous doctrines, both of a docetic tendency, that Chrysostom has in mind in explaining these complex words of Paul. The overtly docetic representatives, personalized by Chrysostom as the Marcionites, use "likeness" to mean phantasm.

Ordinarily, an appeal to the reality of the flesh of Christ would be Chrysostom's stock response, but here he is aware of a need to be more specific, to answer a milder version of docetism. That is the teaching of Apollinaris which excluded a rational soul from the person of Christ. Shortly after this section Chrysostom says: "I must now speak against those who deny that he [Christ] took a soul." His apologetic sights are now specifically trained on Apollinaris, but, surprisingly, his response is one short sentence: "If 'the form of God' is 'perfect God,' then the 'form of a servant' is 'a perfect servant.'" Τέλειος was used in a general way to affirm the perfection of Christ's divinity and humanity by virtually every major writer in the East since Ignatius.[235] But later, and especially after Apollinaris, τέλειος became the standard term by which the idea of incompleteness in Christ's humanity was opposed. Chrysostom is satisfied that a common traditional expression and a simple turn of logic adequately address the problem.

This may seem incredible at first. Apollinaris, teaching in Chrysostom's native Antioch not more than a few decades before Chrysostom, had opened the question of the specific composition of the humanity of Christ more widely than it had ever been before. The later christological controversy is in some sense a continuing reaction to Apollinaris for he had put the spotlight on the soul of Christ, and from then on no christological theory could

---

[235] See the article in Lampe, pp. 1379f.

ignore it. But Apollinaris himself had been decisively silenced. Because of the clear condemnation he received from a council in Rome in 377, synods in Alexandria and Antioch in 378 and 379 respectively, and the council of Constantinople in 381, the church both in the East and in the West was from then on committed to confessing that Christ possessed a real human soul.[236] The fact that Chrysostom mentions Apollinaris' name only once (the sixth homily on Philippians) and explicitly responds to his teaching only once (the seventh homily), may simply indicate how complete the rejection of Apollinaris was.

We also find in this passage from the seventh homily on Philippians the concern Chrysostom had for maintaining the unchanging nature of the Logos. Although the point is fully treated in the next chapter, it suffices to say now in reference to this text that Chrysostom is keenly aware that the assumption by the Logos of a real humanity—soul and body—may seem to imply a change or degeneration in divinity. This is impossible. And so he assures his congregation that whatever else Paul means in this passage, he does not mean that God could have changed in essence.

One other use of ψυχή in reference to Christ, though barely noticeable, occurs in the twenty-seventh homily on John. "For the crucifixion took place," Chrysostom says, "not by reason of the impotence of the Crucified, and not by reason of the superior strength of the Jews; it was because 'God loved the world' that his living temple [ὁ ἔμψυχος αὐτοῦ ναός] was crucified."[237] Ἔμψυχος was sometimes used by the Fathers in conscious opposition to the ideas of Apollinaris,[238] but it may equally well be used simply in the sense of "animated" or "living." It seems more likely that Chrysostom employs the term to contrast the animated Temple

---

[236] Not even Cyril and the Monophysites, though wanting to minimize the activity of the interior human life of Christ, deny that he had a rational soul.

[237] *Hom. in Jn.* 27, 2 (PG 59, 159).

[238] As, for example, Basil: "Our Lord was not soulless flesh, but Godhead using flesh endued with soul [σαρκὶ ἐμψύχῳ]" (*ep.* 236, 1).

with past temples made with stone, than to define the anthropological makeup of Christ.

## Summary

Our intent is to wait until the concluding chapter to make specific comparisons between Chrysostom's Christology and that of writers of his own period. But at this point the following observations may be made regarding his understanding of the humanity of Christ.

1. If maintaining the divinity of Christ against the Eunomians was Chrysostom's greatest theological concern (Chap. 2), then defending his real humanity was a close second. Even before the finer questions are asked about the constitution of Christ's human nature, the fundamental fact that he was human was still in need of defense. Docetic approaches had been repudiated for centuries before Chrysostom's own day, yet there evidently remained in the popular mind the temptation to solve the basic philosophical problem of spirit and matter in a way that sacrifices the material reality of the incarnation.

2. Thus Chrysostom, when he seeks to confirm the reality of the humanity of Christ, echoes the most traditional terminology of the East. The most characteristic expression is the assumed flesh of the Son. Φύσις is used frequently as a direct parallel of σάρξ,[239] and what Chrysostom basically has in mind by "flesh" is simple corporeality. The preacher looks for identifiable standards of orthodoxy by which to instruct his congregation, and the real flesh was the most tangible standard used in the New Testament and by the Fathers. It is important that Christ really hungered and needed rest. But that is not all that "flesh" entails. Chrysostom's aim is to make clear that in the incarnation consubstantiality is achieved, and thus the elevation and enthronement of human

---

[239] E.g. "[Christ was] from the flesh of a Virgin. . . that no one might think that the child was of another nature than ours" (*Hom. in Jn.* 26, 1 [PG 59, 154]). Also, *Hom. in Matt.* 12, 1 (PG 57, 201); ibid. 19, 5 (PG 57, 280); ibid. 44, 3 (PG 57, 467); *Hom. in Heb.* 5, 1 (PG 63, 45-46).

nature. Although Chrysostom does not specifically mention the lower, irrational soul, it may be inferred from his descriptions of the emotional experience of Christ that he held it to be an inevitable consequence of real flesh. He mentions dread of death, for instance, in the same breath with hunger and weariness. It is fair to say, then, that "flesh" means for Chrysostom both body and soul, at least on this level.

3. Chrysostom's direct affirmation of a human soul in Christ and his specific mention of Apollinaris indicates that he was aware of the problems that arise if Christ is not confessed as having a rational soul. But the meager attention he pays to the issue indicates either that Apollinaris' condemnation was so effective in the popular mind that his ideas are no real threat, or that Chrysostom himself did not know how theologically to integrate a rational soul in Christ into his understanding of soteriology, or both. The first possiblity is not unlikely, for by the time Chrysostom begins preaching in Antioch the judgment of the Council of Constantinople against Apollinaris had stood for the better part of a decade and may have been considered by many to have settled the issue. The central issues will not re-emerge until the struggle between Nestorius and Cyril. Given the importance of the teaching posts he occupied both in Antioch and Constantinople, and the relish with which he ordinarily takes apart the ideas of heretics in his sermons, it is most probable that if Chrysostom had seen the church as still threatened by a lingering false doctrine, his references to it would have been frequent and vivid.

But the second possible explanation for Chrysostom's lack of emphasis on the rational soul of Christ seems likely as well. He did not know how to integrate it into his soteriological assumptions. Chrysostom was not alone in both affirming a rational soul in Christ and not including it in a positive way into his soteriological teaching. Even if, as some maintain, Athanasius eventually conceded to theological language that confesses a rational soul, he continues to speak christologically and soteriologically in a way that does not require it.[240] The pattern is later repeated by Cyril. If active obedience of the human nature is not essentially what makes the incarnation efficacious for salvation, then the fullness of the operations of that nature becomes less important.

4. Though Chrysostom depicts the operations of emotion and will as genuinely human, the divinity of Christ predominates. And when it does not it is because the Logos deliberately allows the flesh to be seen as genuine. The picture is not so much that of a freely acting, decision-making ego, as Theodore of Mopsuestia and others of the Antiochene school depicted it, as it is that of the Logos, united to the flesh, providing only at select moments a demonstration of the real flesh. Chrysostom's way of explaining the phenomenon in one such instance, the prayer in Gethsemane, is: "At that time, he left his flesh deserted and stripped of any divine power of operation to show its weakness."[241] In the case of intellect, the predominance of the Logos is even further demonstrated, for Chrysostom never attributes a free human thought to the human nature of Christ. There is always an explanation for seeming ignorance in Christ, and it is never that Christ actually lacked knowledge, even in his flesh.

5. Though Chrysostom sees the human nature of Christ as possessing the same needs and desires as any man, it is not the actual subject of any of the activities in his earthly life. Some aspects may be described "according to the flesh" or "according to the economy" over against other aspects which are "according

---

[240] It has been argued that in his *Tomus ad Antiochenos*, which Athanasius wrote for the Council of Alexandria in 362 he conceded a rational soul in saying that Christ did not have "a body without a soul nor without sense or intelligence" (σῶμα ἄψυχον οὐδ᾽ ἀναίσθητον οὐδ᾽ ἀνόητον). See M. Richard, "Saint Athanase et la psychologie du Christ selon les Ariens," *Mélanges de Science Religieuse* 4 (1947): 5-54. But even this statement may not be a clear admission of a human soul and mind in Christ. Such is the argument of P. Galtier, "Saint Athanse et l'âme humaine du Christ," *Gregorianum* 36 (1955): 553-89; and J. N. D. Kelly, *Early Christian Doctrines*, rev. ed. (New York: Harper & Row, 1978), pp. 288f.

[241] See the discussion above, p. 70.

to the divinity," but Chrysostom is allowing a duality of attribution, not of subjects.

6. Finally, it is obvious how closely aligned to the biblical text Chrysostom is. He uses the terms it presents him with even when it is obvious that they produce theological strain on his presuppositions. In a sense, this makes the interpretation of Chrysostom more challenging, for his own theological syntheses cannot be compared with other theological positions of the period simply by looking at the terms. Some traditional treatments of Chrysostom have come short of an accurate picture for this very reason.[242] Neither can one assume an element is missing because certain non-biblical terms are rare or missing. Chrysostom considered his task to be the illumination of the holy text, and that means not only that bibilical terminology is to be explained, it must be applied. While the same can generally be said of most of the Fathers, its effects are especially evident when the context of almost all the teaching is the bishop's chair and the open book.

---

[242] Note, for instance Eduard Weigl, *Christologie vom Tode des Athanasius bis zum Ausbruch des Nestorianischen Streites* (373-429), Münchener Studien zur historischen Theologie, 4, (Munich, 1925; reprint ed. Hildersheim, 1973), pp. 49-50, whose analysis of Chrysostom in which he depicts him as a classic representative of the Antiochene school is based upon brief quotations from the florilegium *Doctrina patrum de incarnatione verbi*, crit. ed. by F. Diekamp (Münster, 1907), some of which are from spurious works. The longest and most important quotation is from the spurious letter to Caesarius.

## Chapter Four

# Chrysostom on the Incarnation

### The Incarnation as Divine Economy

Christology and soteriology are inseparable theological themes in the ancient East and the place of their conjunction is the incarnation of Christ. The use of οἰκονομία by various Greek authors ranges from the idea of administration and ordering to the cosmic plan of God. It was natural, then, that the Greek Fathers would use οἰκονομία to describe the high point of salvation history—the incarnation. The divine οἰκονομία as incarnation is, for Chrysostom, the most crucial theological issue, for it is the foundation of the salvation offered to the race. It also presents human beings with the greatest enigma of the faith, for the union of uncreated divine nature with created human nature is a conception held only with the greatest possible strain on common metaphysical assumptions. That a nature ἄτρεπτος should come into contact with, even mingle with, a nature τρεπτός was necessary but remains to us a mystery. Chrysostom frequently instructs his congregation on the proper understanding of this doctrine so surrounded with potential pitfalls, as, for example, when he comes to Jn. 1:14, "and the Word became flesh," or Phil. 2:7, which says Christ took the form of a servant and was made in human likeness. If the incarnation is the greatest mystery of the faith, it also presents its greatest difficulty: how can divinity be united to humanity without a change or degeneration of its own nature?

The fourth-century response to this dilemma has often been categorized by modern interpreters into two fundamentally different views. The first is that the humanity of Christ, though real, is not substantial enough to present any kind of metaphysical challenge to the divinity of Christ. If there is really only one determining nature in the incarnate Christ, then that divine and unchangable nature remains unmixed. What is comforting to Cyril and others from Alexandria, however, is disappointing to the likes of Theodore of Mopsuestia and Nestorius. They insist on a fuller human nature in Christ, and thus their solution to the dilemma takes an entirely different turn. It is the ontological and experiential distinctness of the two natures that, for them, guarantees the completeness and integrity of both natures. In this case it is the unity of Christ's person that is perhaps compromised.

In the homilies of John Chrysostom we find a Christology that bears some of the characteristics of both positions. Rowan Greer, in his examination of fourth-century soteriology,[243] concludes from Chrysostom's homilies on Hebrews that he does not fit the traditional "Antiochene" mold as regards Christology, not because he is more "Alexandrian," but because his terminology has confused the two. The objective behind this chapter is to see if Chrysostom's thought on the relationship between the natures of Christ is coherent. The thesis defended here is that there is indeed such a coherence, that Chrysostom is aware of the dual problem of the unity of Christ and the completeness of the natures, and that an important category he uses for reaching such a synthesis is his understanding of the incarnation as condescension.

### The Meaning of οἰκονομία

One cannot appreciate Chrysostom's Christology without understanding the content of οἰκονομία as he uses the term. It occurs most often when Chrysostom is explaining the incarnation,

---

[243] Greer, *The Captain of our Salvation: a Study in the Patristic Exegesis of Hebrews* (Tübingen, 1973).

and, in particular, when he is making a distinction between Christ as divine and the incarnate Christ. As will be noted when the appropriate passages are examined, this distinction is not, strictly speaking, a contrasting of the divine and the human in Christ, but of the pre-incarnate Christ and the incarnate Christ. Something new occurs with the event of the incarnation. It is not the mere juxtaposition of two disparate natures; neither is it the modification of the primary, divine nature. When pure divinity and real humanity come together in the incarnation, humankind is afforded the vehicle for its salvation. A real union has occurred, and a permanent one. Thus, some things can be said of this incarnate Christ—Christ "according to the οἰκονομία"—that cannot be said of the "pure nature" of Christ as Chrysostom likes to call it.

The term οἰκονομία has several distinct meanings in fourth-century Greek.[244] This noun and its verb counterpart οἰκονομέω generally relate to management, governing, or administering. Thus the terms may be used to describe Judas' responsibility as treasurer,[245] or the giving of alms or the alms themselves.[246] They may be used in reference to ecclesiastical administration[247] or the appointment of deacons to assist bishops.[248]

On a higher level, οἰκονομία was used to describe God's providential ordering of life, as Prestige puts it, "administration implies method, and thus 'economy' acquired the sense of plan and design. . . . A word with such a range of associations was extremely apt for adoption as an expression of the providential order. It covers either such gifts as God sends and supplies in a

---

[244] See Prestige, *God in Patristic Thought*, pp. 57-68 from whom much of the background here discussed is borrowed. Also: J. Reumann, "'Stewards of God'– Pre-Christian Religious Application of *Oikonomos* in Greek," *Journal of Biblical Literature* 77 (1958): 339-49.

[245] *Hom. in Jn.* 65, 2 (PG 59, 363).

[246] Origen, *Comm. in Jn.* 19, 7.

[247] Basil, *ep.* 144.

[248] Epiphanius, *Haer.* 75, 4.

providential manner, or such events as He designs and disposes."[249] What is included in God's οἰκονομία may be great or small, cosmic or mundane. It may include the translation of the Septuagint[250] or the order of the lectionary.[251] Chrysostom sees οἰκονομία in the way God used the star of Bethlehem to guide the Magi, and even in God's use of heathen prophets and the witch of Endor to his own purposes.[252]

Because God's providence is ultimately his grace, οἰκονομία becomes a common way of describing the varied and specific ways that grace has been dispensed to the human race. God's covenant or dispensation is evident in the sacraments. So Gregory of Nyssa can say of baptism, "the invocation by prayer, then, which precedes this divine οἰκονομία constitutes an abundance of proof that what is effected is done by God."[253] Epiphanius sometimes calls the Eucharist "the economy of worship."[254] God's grace is also described as οἰκονομία in reference to prophecy and revelation. Origen, for instance, sees in the Scriptures a revelation of mystical economies.[255]

### The Incarnation as οἰκονομία

The greatest act of covenant grace is the incarnation. Prestige says, "the supreme instance of divine economy, whether in the sense of dispensation, condescension, or special providence, was exhibited in the incarnation, for which the word 'oekonomia,' without any verbal qualification, is the regular patristic term from the third century onwards."[256] As such, it is virtually synonymous

---

[249] Prestige, *God in Patristic Thought*, pp. 58-59.

[250] Eusebius, *Preparatio evangelica* 8, 1.

[251] Cyril of Jerusalem, *Catech.* 14, 24.

[252] *Hom. in Matt.* 6, 2 (PG 57, 63); ibid. 6, 3 (PG 57,65).

[253] *Or. catech.* 34.

[254] E.g. *Haer.* 75, 3.

[255] *De principiis* 4, 2, 2.

[256] Prestige, *God in Patristic Thought*, p. 67.

with ἐνανθρώπησις and similar terms.[257] Chrysostom is no exception. The term οἰκονομία is a constant favorite with him; he uses it with regularly in both secular and theological senses.

One detects in Chrysostom's use of οἰκονομία as a description of the incarnation at least three different levels of specificity: 1) οἰκονομία as the incarnation itself; 2) as the unique nature of the Logos after his union with flesh; and 3) as the flesh itself. On the most general level οἰκονομία is the sum total of the gospel. It is the gospel. So, in reference to Matthew's description of itself as a "book of the generation of Jesus Christ," Chrysostom says:

> This book has not the birth only, but the whole οἰκονομία. Because this is the sum of the whole οἰκονομία, and is made an origin and root of all our blessings.[258]

The entire event of Christ's coming is the ultimate manifestation of the economy of God, and incorporates the beginning and the completion of salvation.

Secondly, Chrysostom uses οἰκονομία to refer to the unique nature of the Logos after he became flesh: Christ considered κατὰ τῆς οἰκονομίας. This is Chrysostom's favorite phrase for differentiating the attributes and activities of the eternal Logos and the enfleshed Logos, his way of constantly reminding his congregation that they cannot expect that every attribution in the Scriptures concerning Christ applies purely to the eternal nature of the divine Word, for after the οἰκονομία Christ is different. This is what Arians do not take into account, nor the followers of Paul of Samosata, Marcellus of Ancyra, and others.

---

[257] Note such uses as early as Justin: "those from whom the Christ should arise, according to the economy, through the Virgin Mary" (*Dial.* 120, 1); and Irenaeus (*Haer.* 1, 15, 3) where he describes the gnostic doctrine which saw the birth through Mary as "a special economy."

[258] *Hom. in Matt.* 2, 3 (PG 57, 27). The οἰκονομία includes the specific events of the incarnation. The statement in Hebrews that "through death [Christ] might destroy him that had the power of death," is a description of "the cause of the economy" (*Hom. in Heb.* 4, 4 [PG 63, 41]).

And finally, because the actual uniqueness of this οἰκονομία is the taking of human flesh, the term is used, narrowly, to refer to the flesh of Christ itself. This and the use of οἰκονομία discussed just previously have led some to translate it simply as "human nature" or some such equivalent. But this translation may be questioned on the basis of the fact that when Chrysostom speaks of "Christ κατὰ τῆς οἰκονομίας" he is not necessarily excluding the divinity of Christ. Matthew's depiction of Christ in Gethsemane, for instance, is that of "Christ κατὰ τῆς οἰκονομίας," but the divine nature is not uninvolved. As was shown in the previous chapter, no incident of seeming ignorance, weakness, or suffering in the life of Christ is purely the consequence of a freely acting human nature.

Chrysostom is by no means unusual in using οἰκονομία at these various levels. He is, in fact, using a term uniquely modified by Christians as early as the second century to describe the unusual qualities of the incarnation. This fact in itself is one more reason to see in Chrysostom's use of such terminology the more or less common Greek patristic emphasis on union in the incarnate Christ, rather than the more specialized "Antiochene" emphasis on distinctions. As will be discussed later, the strong distinctions Chrysostom does make with regard to Christ considered "according to the economy" and "according to the divinity" is more a defense against extreme Arianism than an appeal for the complete integrity of the human nature of Christ.

### The Relationship Between the Natures of Christ

The issues hotly contested in the decades immediately after Chrysostom's career are not really about the existence of different natures in Christ, but of the relationship between them. Terms are being forged in these years that will eventually be reflected in the Chalcedonian definition, but even then not unchallenged. In Chrysostom's sermons there are some attempts at setting boundaries for understanding the relationship between the natures. But more important, perhaps, are his explanations of the theological problems that arise from gospel sayings and other Scripture passages, particularly the book of Hebrews, which put Christ in roles that seem less than divine. The title "Son of Man" and the role of high priest, for instance, do not seem completely appropriate for the eternal Logos, and so Chrysostom explains them on the basis of the unique characteristics of the οἰκονομία. It seems that Chrysostom's comprehensive understanding of the relationship of divinity and humanity in Christ includes not only a concern to maintain the union of the two, but also an awareness that unless some distinctions are drawn, one of two vital realities may be compromised: the integrity of the divine nature of the eternal Logos, or the genuineness of the incarnation itself.

## Explicit Definitions

It will probably be most helpful to begin with those few texts in which Chrysostom uses specific and detailed terminology to express the relationship between the divinity and the humanity of Christ. One of the two important texts here examined comes from Chrysostom's earlier career in Antioch and the other from his later preaching in Constantinople. The earlier example occurs in the homilies on John in response to that famous Johannine phrase "and the Word became flesh and dwelt among us." The preacher's concern, of course, is that no one interpret the expression to mean that divine nature was transformed in any way. Here is where the metaphor of indwelling is more helpful than problematic.

> For I did not mean a change of that unchangable nature but its dwelling and habitation. That which dwells cannot be the same thing as its dwelling, but must be something different [ἕτερον]. One thing dwells in another; otherwise the latter would not be a dwelling, for nothing dwells in itself. However, by "different" I mean different in substance [οὐσίαν]. By their union [ἑνώσει] and conjoining [συναφείᾳ], God, the Word, and the flesh are one, not as a result of commingling [συγχύσεως] or disappearance of substances [οὐσιῶν], but by some ineffable and

inexplicable union [ἐνώσεως]. But do not seek the how; it "was made" in a way which he himself knows.[259]

Chrysostom does not often resort to a list of terms to describe the boundaries of his christological understanding, but when he does, as in this example, he uses those that would become standard in fifth-century discussions. Chrysostom possesses, even relatively early in his career, the awareness of the dual problems of confusion and separation of the natures of Christ. For example, he here uses ἔνωσις, one of the strongest terms used to express union. Later writers will carefully qualify the term—thus, one finds the idea of union by favor or grace (ἔνωσις κατ᾿ εὐδοκίαν) in Theodoret and Theodore of Mopsuestia in their attempt to avoid positing a "natural" union, but, in contrast, "hypostatic union" (ἔνωσις καθ᾿ ὑπόστασιν) in Cyril because he sees the union as occuring at the most essential level.

But Chrysostom also describes the coming together of the Word and its dwelling as συνάφεια, conjunction. With both terms, then—ἔνωσις, commonly associated with the Alexandrians, and συνάφεια, with the Antiochenes—Chrysostom attempts to define the fundamental fact that "God, the Word, and the flesh are one." Chrysostom is just as aware as other pre-Chaledonian Greek theologians like the Cappadocians that a doctrine of two Sons must be avoided. But there is lacking the fineness of distinction between terms like ἔνωσις and συνάφεια which later debates will produce. Chrysostom refuses to carry the speculation further than to say that an "ineffable and inexplicable union" exists in the Son.

---

[259] *Hom. in Jn.* 11, 2 (PG 59, 80). This is the text used by the Council of Chalcedon. The Greek of the entire passage reads as follows: Οὐ γὰρ τροπὴν εἶπον τῆς ἀτρέπτου φύσεως ἐκείνης, ἀλλὰ σκήνωσιν καὶ κατοίκησιν. Τὸ δὲ σκηνοῦν, οὐ ταὐτὸν ἂν εἴη τῇ σκηνῇ, ἀλλ᾿ ἕτερον. "Ετερον γὰρ ἐν ἑτέρῳ σκηνοῖ· ἐπεὶ οὐδ᾿ ἂν εἴη σκήνωσις· οὐδὲν γὰρ ἐν ἑαυτῷ κατοικεῖ. "Ετερον δὲ εἶπον κατὰ τὴν οὐσίαν. Τῇ γὰρ ἑνώσει καὶ τῇ συναφείᾳ ἕν ἐστιν ὁ Θεὸς Λόγος καὶ ἡ σάρξ, οὐ συγχύσεως γενομένης, οὐδὲ ἀφανισμοῦ τῶν οὐσιῶν, ἀλλ᾿ ἑνώσεως ἀρρήτου τινὸς καὶ ἀφράστου. Τὸ δὲ ὅπως, μὴ ζήτει· ἐγένετο γὰρ ὡς οἶδεν αὐτός.

He sees the problems, but is content to leave the "how" to the mind of God himself.

Where this text begins is not with the union, but with the strong assertion of the distinctness of the Word and its dwelling. Chrysostom here sees the dwelling metaphor as a most convenient qualification of the Word's "becoming" flesh—a dwelling is different (ἕτερον) from what indwells it. Gregory of Nazianzus had similarly used simple adjectives to distinguish the human and the divine in Christ: "the Savior is made of elements which are distinct from one another [ἄλλο καὶ ἄλλο], for the invisible is not the same as the visible, nor the timeless with that which is subject to time." But Gregory is quick to add: "But there is not one Person [ἄλλος] and another Person [ἄλλος]."[260]

When Chrysostom similarly qualifies his assertion of the distinctness of divinity and its dwelling, he goes further than Gregory in the language he uses. That which indwells is different from its dwelling κατὰ τὴν οὐσίαν. The extremes of the Apollinarian position required an assertion of a singular οὐσία in Christ.[261] Neither substance disappears [ἀφανισμοῦ] in their uniting. Yet once again the σάρξ terminology ("God, the Word, and the σάρξ are one") raises the question of the nature of the human οὐσία to which the Word was united. As has been previously discussed,[262] Chrysostom uses σάρξ as a description of the humanity in Christ which includes primarily physical, but also emotional characteristics, while excluding the autonomy and integrity of a fully-functioning mind and will. What does not "disappear," in other words, is the fleshly Son of Man, who, because he is real flesh, could die a real human death. Ambiguity remains as to whether the "dwelling" ever was an οὐσία functioning distinctly from the Λόγος.

---

[260] *Ep.* 101.

[261] E. g. *Fr.* 158: οὐκ ἐν δύο οὐσίαις ἀλλ ἐν μιᾷ.

[262] Cf. Chap. 3, pp. 109-22.

Neither does the union and conjunction of the Word and its dwelling imply σύγχυσις, commingling. It had already become common to reject trinitarian heresies like Sabellianism on the basis that they involved a σύγχυσις of the hypostases of the Father and the Son.[263] Likewise the term came into christological discussions as a description of a mistaken notion of the union of the natures. The Antiochenes understood Cyril's hypostatic union as nothing other than a confusion, σύγχυσις, of natures.[264]

Another key commentary of Chrysostom's occurs in his exposition of a pivotal text for the doctrine of the incarnation, Phil. 2, and especially the phrase "being found in the form of a man." The passage raises the question whether any distinction can be made between what the Logo" "became" and what he "took." Chrysostom does indeed find such a distinction in these terms.

> The Word who was God did not degenerate [μετέπεσεν] into man, nor was His substance changed [μετεβλήθη], but he appeared [ἐφάνη] as a man; not to delude us with a phantom, but to instruct us in humility. When therefore he says, "as a man," this is what he means; since he calls him a man elsewhere also, when he says, "there is one God, one Mediator also between God and men, himself man, Christ Jesus".... Again, against the Arians. Here concerning His divinity [περὶ τῆς θεότητος], we no longer find "he became," "he took," but "he emptied himself, taking the form of a servant, being made in the likeness of men"; here concerning his humanity [περὶ τῆς ἀνθρωπότητος] we find "he took, he became." He became [ἐγένετο] the latter, he took [ἔλαβεν] the latter; he was [ὑπῆρχε] the former. Let us not then confound [συγχέωμεν] nor divide [διϊστῶμεν] [the natures]. There is one God, there is one Christ, the Son of God. When I say "one," I

---

[263] For example, Basil, *Ep.* 224, 2: "I anathematize all who hold the vile opinion of the confusion (σύγχυσις) of the hypostases, on which point the most impious heresy of Sabellius has been revived."

[264] So Theodoret charges Cyril with Apollinarianism: "He brings in the hypostatic union, and a meeting by natural union, and by these terms he represents that a kind of mixture and confusion (σύγχυσις) was effected of the divine nature and of the form of the servant. This comes of the innovation of the Apollinarian heresy" (*ep.* 151).

mean a union [ἕνωσιν], not a confusion [σύγχυσιν]; the one nature did not degenerate [μεταπεσούσης] into the other, but was united [ἡνωμένης] with it.[265]

Sellers observes that the discomfort many of the Antiochenes had with Jn. 1:14 ("the Word became flesh"), the locus classicus of the Alexandrians, resulted in a different locus classicus, "the Word took flesh."[266] Chrysostom shows here in his commentary on Phil. 2 a willingness to say of the Word, not just that he "took" [ἔλαβεν] flesh, but also that he "became" [ἐγένετο] flesh. However, he is quick to point out Paul's use of ὑπῆρχε to express the original nature of the Son—"he existed in the form of God" (Phil. 2:6). The Word took flesh, he even became flesh, but it is more proper to say that he was divinity. One might suspect that Chrysostom, like later Antiochenes, is trying to minimize the thought that the Word actually became anything. "Becoming" only means "taking," and that is ultimately a condition that leaves essential being untouched. But Chrysostom is probably not using ὑπάρχω, a term generally connected with existence "from the beginning," in order to minimize the meaning of γίνομαι, but to make a distinction of time between what the Word was from the beginning, and what he became in the incarnation. Here is Christology defined by existential verbs. If Chrysostom makes a point of the distinction of natures in Christ, as is apparent from this and many other texts, it is more a distinction of the nature of the Word before the incarnation and the nature of the Word after his uniting with flesh. Such is the meaning of the concluding phrase: "when I say 'one,' I mean a union, not a confusion; the one nature did not degenerate into the other, but was united with it."

---

[265] *Hom. in Phil.* 8 (Field 5, 41).

[266] Note, for example, Theodore: "The word 'became' can be interpreted only as meaning 'according to appearance'.... In appearance the Logos became flesh, and by 'appearance' we mean, not that the Logos did not take real flesh, but that he did not 'become' flesh. For when the Scripture says he 'took,' it means that he took not in appearance but in truth. But when it says he 'became,' then it is speaking 'according to appearance'; for he was not transformed into flesh" (*De Incarn.* 9, fr. 2; cited by Sellers, *Two Ancient Christologies*, p. 182).

This is the same kind of distinction Athanasius and even Apollinaris made.[267] It is obvious that the Logos before the incarnation was somehow different than after the enfleshment. It is only before the incarnation that the Logos may be considered wholly apart from any other nature, i. e. that his "pure nature" may be identified. Because the union with flesh was real, the Logos after the incarnation is the Logos "according to the economy."

### The Unity of Christ and the *Communicatio Idiomatum*

Long before a terminology of unity was sought by Greek theologians, the unity of Christ's person was expressed by attributing characteristics of one nature to the other nature. So, to speak of God being born of a Virgin or of God suffering was to say that in the incarnation divinity has been substantially joined with humanity. Though widespread in popular usage,[268] such expressions did not necessarily come easily for Greek teachers of the fourth century. J. N. D. Kelly says of Gregory of Nyssa, for instance, that even when he called the Virgin "Theotokos," "he seems to have been making a concession to popular usage, and the customary language of the *communicatio idiomatum* about God's suffering, dying, etc., clearly did not come naturally to his lips."[269] Eventually the *communicatio idiomatum* (the "interchange of properties," ἀντίδοσις τῶν ἰδιωμάτων) became the substance of controversy as Nestorius rejected the use of theotokos and his opponents made it the mark of orthodoxy.

---

[267] For instance, both Athanasius and Apollinaris think it necessary to say that "God suffered," and "God died," but only of the divinity that had become flesh. Such statements would never be said of the Logos in his pre-incarnate, eternal being. Athanasius at one point makes use of 1 Pet. 4:1, "Christ therefore suffered in the flesh," in order to show that real passions are "natural properties not of the Logos but of the flesh" (*Contra Arianos* 3, 34).

[268] So, for instance, as early as Ignatius are found expressions like "the blood of God," "the suffering of my God," and "God . . . was conceived in Mary" (*Eph.* 1, 1; 18, 2; *Rom.* 6, 3).

[269] J. N. D. Kelly, *Early Christian Doctrines*, p.300.

In Chrysostom we find someone who uses the traditional expressions, but only occasionally, and oftentimes accompanied by qualifications designed to answer anyone who would use the *communicatio idiomatum* to deny that Christ really became man. The kind of statement that follows is one such example of the *communicatio idiomatum* used with a fair degree of self-consciousness:

> It is far beyond all thought to hear that God the Unspeakable [ἀπόρρητος], the Unutterable [ἀνέκφραστος], the Incomprehensible [ἀπερινόητος], and he that is equal to the Father, has passed through a virgin's womb and has vouchsafed to be born of a woman, and to have Abraham and David for forefathers.[270]

Speaking of the adoration of the Magi, Chrysostom says: "Let Marcion be ashamed, beholding God worshipped in the flesh."[271] The thrust of such expressions is anti-Arian. But Chrysostom is also aware that it is precisely the seeming self-contradictory nature of these expressions that provided the Neo-Arians with some of their most cogent arguments. God, in his essence, cannot be born, and he certainly cannot suffer. Thus, they reasoned, Christ could not be God. The use of *communicatio idiomatum* may, in other words, create more problems than it solves. Chrysostom prefers a tactic of demonstration and proof of the divinity of Christ, and thus uses such expressions relatively infrequently.

Even though Chrysostom shows caution in using the *communicatio idiomatum*, he does clearly endorse the principle. Chrysostom struggles with the statement that the Son was given his disciples by the Father (Jn. 17:6). How could the divine Son have to receive anything, especially in the light of his oneness with the Father? It is spoken in condescension to the weakness of the listeners, but "this cannot be said of the Son merely as man, but only insofar as he has a nature greater than that of a man, for it is

---

[270] *Hom. in Matt.* 2, 2 (PG 57, 25).

[271] Ὁρῶν Θεὸν ἐν σαρκὶ προσκυνούμενον (Hom. in Matt. 7, 4 [PG 57, 77]).

clearly evident to all that what belongs to the lesser nature belongs also to the greater, but the opposite is not the case."[272] The point is this: to speak of the Son receiving from the Father is more a human manner of speaking than divine, but since it cannot be predicated of the Son merely as man, it must refer to Christ as both divine and human. In the unity of the person of the Son an interchange of properties exists.[273] The principle again comes out in a discussion about the phrase "thou art my Son, this day have I begotten thee": "For indeed the flesh partakes of the high things, just as the Godhead of the lowly [καὶ γὰρ ἡ σάρξ κοινωνεῖ τῶν ὑψηλῶν, ὡσπεροῦν καὶ ἡ θεότης τῶν ταπεινῶν]. For he who disdained not to become man, and did not decline the reality [πρᾶγμα], how should he have declined the expressions [τὰ ῥήματα]?"[274]

## Distinctions of Attribution

The question of the relationship between the natures of Christ is in large part the question of distinctions made between those natures. All but the most extreme monophysite voices of the fourth and fifth centuries drew some distinctions between the divine and human manifestations of Christ. Some used distinctions at the most superficial level: "humanity" and "divinity" as the two faces of Christ who was really one hypostasis. Those at the opposite extreme made distinctions so complete as to specify a "manhood" of Christ which was a

---

[272] Τὸ μὲν γὰρ τοῦ ἐλάττονος, ὅτι τοῦ μείζονός ἐστι, παντί του δῆλου· τὸ δὲ ἔμπαλιν, οὐκέτι (*Hom. in Jn.* 81, 1 [PG 59, 339]).

[273] Chrysostom makes a similar point while explaining how the title "Son of man," assumed to be a more human title, could be used in reference to Jesus' heavenly origin. "He did not mean only his humanity by "the Son of man," but here called his entire person [τὸ πᾶν], so to speak, by the name of the lesser part. And I say this, for it was his custom frequently to name the whole from his Godhead, and as often to name it from his humanity" (*Hom. in Jn.* 27, 1 [PG 59, 158]).

[274] *Hom. in Heb.* 2, 3 (PG 63, 25).

hypostasis in its own right and carried with it all the human frailties and limitations endemic to the race.

It is in the treatment of biblical texts which attribute to Christ what seem to be less than divine characteristics that the monophysites[275] are presented with the greatest challenge to the unity of Christ and the dyophysites with the best evidence that there really are two distinct φύσεις.[276] It is not surprising, then, that in the hundreds of biblical homilies of Chrysostom there are numerous occasions for comment on the kinds of distinctions that may be drawn. The gospels inevitably raise the issue, but even more so, in Chrysostom's treatment, the book of Hebrews. It is Hebrews perhaps more than any other New Testament book that specifies the mediatorial salvific functions of the incarnate Christ, functions that Chrysostom sees as special attributes of the incarnate, not the eternal, nature of Christ. His anointing, his intercession, his high priesthood, and certainly his suffering, are all set in a separate category from his eternal characteristics. The question is whether Chrysostom, in making such distinctions, is describing Christ as ontologically or functionally diverse.

This question must always be raised in any examination of fourth-century Christology because the fact that a particular theologian makes distinctions between the humanity and divinity of Christ does not necessarily imply a dyophysite understanding. Distinctions of attribution are not necessarily ontological distinctions. The importance of this difference must be emphasized, for we find in fourth and fifth-century Christologies much common ground as far as expressions are concerned. Virtually everyone recognizes the validity and necessity of

---

[275] The term "monophysite" is used here not specifically with reference to the fifth-century opponents of Chalcedon, but as a general description of any who saw in Christ only one real principle of operation. "Dyophysite" indicates the tendency to make a real, not just verbal, distinction of natures.

[276] This point is fundamental to Rowan Greer's interpretation of Theodore of Mopsuestia in which he sees Theodore's strong dyophysite tendencies as the natural consequence of Theodore's strong adherence to the biblical text. *Theodore of Mopsuestia: Exegete and Theologian* (London, 1961).

distinguishing Christ "as God" from Christ "as man."[277] But there is a fundamental difference between understanding that distinction as a way of regarding Christ as opposed to a definition of the essential being of Christ. By Chrysostom's time the practice of "recognizing the natures" was a well established way of acknowledging a revealed duality in Christ while stopping short of positing an essential duality.[278] These are the concepts of Christologies less developed but safer than those of the fifth century.

Special functions of the incarnate nature of Christ and their implications for Christology in general will be treated in the next section, but first we will take note of a few texts that specifically describe the distinction of the human and the divine. The Pentecost sermon of Peter in Acts 2 contains the controversial statement concerning Christ that God "made him Lord and Christ." In response to the problem of Christ being made something Chrysostom says:

> Are you ignorant that some of the words are said of his pure nature [τῆς ἀκηράτου φύσεως], others of his incarnate nature [τῆς οἰκονομίας]. If this is not so, but you interpret all absolutely as referring to the Godhead, you will also conclude that God can suffer. But, if he cannot suffer, he was not created.

---

[277] The anti-Arian polemic required it. Note Athanasius' application of the principle: "If we recognize what is proper to each, and see and understand that both these things and those are done by One, we are right in our faith and shall never stray. But if a man looking at what is done divinely by the Word, deny the body, or looking at what is proper to the body, deny the Word's presence in the flesh, or from what is human entertain low thoughts concerning the Word, such a one, as a Jewish vintner, mixing water with the wine, shall account the cross an offence, or as a Gentile, will deem the preaching folly. This then is what happens to God's enemy the Arians" (*Contra Arianos* 3, 26).

[278] Again, note Athanasius: "For so long as we are confessing that he became man there is no question about saying. . . whether 'he became,' or 'he has been made,' or 'created,' or 'formed,' or 'servant,' or 'son of a handmaid,' or 'son of man,' or 'was constituted,' or 'took his journey,' or 'bridegroom,' or 'brother's son,' or 'brother.' All these terms happen to be proper to man's constitution; and such as these do not designate the essence of the Word, but that he has become man" (*Contra Arianos* 2, 14).

If blood flowed from the deity itself and its ineffable nature [ἀρρήτου φύσεως], and if it were pierced and cut by nails, instead of Christ's flesh, in the crucifixion, your fallacy would therefore be reasonable. . . . The words "Lord" and "Christ" are not used of his essence [οὐσίας] but of his rank [ἀξιώματος]; the one refers to his power [ἐξουσίας], the other to his anointing [χρισθῆναι].[279]

The distinction, succinctly put here, is between a "pure nature" and an "incarnate nature." Chrysostom sees "Lord" and "Christ" in Acts 2:36 as applying specifically to the incarnate nature of Christ which he further defines as "rank" and "anointing." It is clear that Chrysostom is speaking in functional rather than ontological categories, of the position in salvation history which the Logos took when he became clothed with flesh. In fact "rank" or "dignity" becomes a favorite term with Chrysostom when he wants to refer to the special characteristics of the incarnate Christ. On the other hand, to consider Christ in his "pure nature" is to regard his "essence" or "power." Now functional definitions have given way to the ontological. No doubt οὐσία was the existential term in Chrysostom's vocabulary most suitable to describe the innermost essence of being, and ἐξουσία, a term not so widely used in speculative theology but central to the biblical descriptions of the eternal Son, reinforces the same point.

The duality of natures in this and other passages is a twofold depiction of Christ as, first and foremost, the eternal Logos, and secondarily the Logos under the special conditions of the incarnation. The incarnate Christ has taken real human nature, as is evidenced in his physical needs and suffering, but Christ remains one person, even one acting principle, despite the assumption of humanity.

In another text Chrysostom discusses the problem of duality and unity in Christ:

I have never left the assumed humanity unharmonized with the divine operation [οὐδαμοῦ τὴν ἀναληφθεῖσαν ἀνθρωπότητα

---

[279] *Hom. in Jn.* 3, 3 (PG 59, 41).

τῆς θείας ἐνεργείας ἄμικτον ἀπολέλοιπα], (acting) now as man, now as God, both indicating the nature, and bringing faith to the economy; teaching that the humbler things are to be referred to the humanity, and the nobler to the divinity, and by this unequal mixture of actions, interpreting the unequal union of the natures [διὰ τῆς ἀνίσου ταύτης τῶν ἔργων κράσεως τὴν ἄνισον τῶν φύσεων ἕνωσιν ἑρμηνεύων], and by (my) power over sufferings, declaring that my own sufferings are voluntary; as God, I curbed nature, supporting a fast for forty days, but afterwards, as man, I was hungry and tired; as God, I calmed the raging sea, as man, I was tempted by the devil; as God, I expelled devils, as man, I am about to suffer for men.[280]

Grillmeier's comment on this important text emphasizes the non-Antiochene elements present in it: "We can hardly go far wrong in seeing behind formulas like this the Stoic principle of 'predominance' and also a Stoic krasis-doctrine. We are far from a picture of Christ like that given by Theodore of Mopsuestia."[281] Chrysostom here defines the perspective he brings to the many biblical texts that show God acting in human form—the humanity must be seen as real, but must not be in any real sense competitive with the divinity. The parallelism of ἕνωσις and κρᾶσις suggests, as Grillmeier says, that in the union Chrysostom understands the divine nature to be the truly active subject. Chrysostom may, like the Antiochenes, assign different verses in the gospels variously to Christ as man and as God, but, like the Alexandrians, mean no more in this than that the divine Christ allows the attributes of weak and frail humanity to be demonstrated in his incarnate life. This is not docetic, for the humanity is real. But by the same token the divinity always predominates. There is, then, a duality of natures, but an "unequal union of natures," resulting, not surprisingly, in an "unequal mixture of actions."

---

280 *In quatrid. Lazarum* 1 (PG 50, 642-43), cited by Hay.
281 Grillmeier, *Christ in Christian Tradition*, p. 420.

The Special Functions of the Incarnate Nature

Chrysostom's understanding of the relationship between the natures of Christ is revealed in a somewhat different way when he has occasion to treat those biblical statements that apply to Christ attributes or activities that seem less than eternal. These are difficulties in Chrysostom's theology because of his concern to maintain the predominance of the divine nature of Christ while giving credibility to those roles which Christ assumes in the incarnation. The passages may be categorized into three types: those which envision Christ's identification with human experience; those which imply any kind of change, and those which describe his mediatorial roles which are the special consequences of the economy of God in the broad sense. In the first category belong any assertions of suffering, temptation, or any human need in the God-man; in the second biblical expressions like "being made," or "anointed," and the like; and in the third any functions like intercession or priesthood which, in Chrysotom's mind, place Christ between God and man. It is in these areas that we often see the differences of approach of the Antiochene and Alexandrian approaches, but Chrysostom presents something of a mixed view in that he sees all such attributes belonging to the incarnate nature of Christ, but not merely to his manhood. Here we have further indications that when Chrysostom attributes a particular biblical event or description to the οἰκονομία or to the "humanity" of Christ, he does not so much mean a human nature distinguished from a divine as much as the united, incarnate nature distinguished from the pre-incarnate, eternal Word.

The issue of identification with human experience arises primarily in gospel texts where one finds a picture of Christ as sometimes fleeing, sometimes dreading death, and sometimes even calling out in prayer. What, for instance, could John have possibly meant by saying that Jesus "could not" move about in Judea because the Jews were seeking to put him to death?

O blessed John, what are you saying? Is it that he who was able to do anything whatsoever he willed "could not"?.... He [John] did this to make it clear that at one time Christ's divinity was being attested, at another, his humanity. When he said, "he could not," he was speaking of him as a man [ὡς περὶ ἀνθρώπου] who did many things even in a human way [ἀνθρωπίνως], but when he asserted that he stood in their midst and they did not seize him, he was, of course, proving the power of his Godhead. And this is so for in fleeing Christ was acting as man, and in making his appearance he was acting as God; in both cases, genuinely. The fact that he was not seized even though surrounded by those who were plotting against him was proof of his invincibility and inviolability, while his withdrawal confirmed and strengthened the doctrine of the incarnation [οἰκονομίαν], so that Paul of Samosata might have nothing to say, or Marcion, or those infected with the disease of their teachings.[282]

Chrysostom is here in typical fashion walking the narrow path between the two troubling propositions that Christ really was subject to the malicious will of human beings or that he only appeared to be in danger, the antithetical "diseases" of Paul of Samosata and Marcion. Such experiences affirm the doctrine of the incarnation in that a total identification with humanity is demonstrated, yet the question must be raised whether by this Chrysostom means that the humanity is acting here in isolation from the divinity. It is just as likely that Chrysostom's "as man—as God" terminology is descriptive of the phenomenon of incarnation, not of the ontological conditions necessary to ensure a full humanity.

Chrysostom similarly attributes the passion of Christ and the dread of it to the economy. The "as man—as God" comparison occurs in the discussion of Christ's Gethsemane prayer: "In those places in which he foretells his passion and desires that it come to pass, he speaks as God; but, as man, he shuns it and prays to

---

[282] *Hom. in Jn.* 48, 1 (PG 59, 269).

avert it."[283] The degree to which Chrysostom here intends to portray the humanity as distinct from the divinity is indicated by an expression in this same homily: "At that time, he left his flesh deserted and stripped of any divine power of operation to show its weakness and to confirm its nature. At other times, he conceals it so that you may know that he is not merely a man." Two important assumptions are exposed in this kind of analysis: first, divinity predominates over humanity; and second, humanity and divinity may be distinguished in Christ, but the humanity in such distinctions is limited to the flesh. The incarnation requires a real body, but God is not a body. Such a distinction therefore is far from controversial, something that could not be said of the distinctions made by Theodore of Mopsuestia and others. It is indeed nothing more than the ancient metaphysical axiom of the opposition of flesh and spirit, whereas Theodore was proposing a distinction of spiritual principles in Christ. Passion, then, is a distinctly human characteristic of the incarnation and as such invites a distinction of human and divine when such expressions are encountered. But, because in Chrysostom's understanding the reality of the passion of Christ is seated in the reality of his σάρξ, he comes short of a Word-Man type Christology.

Essentially the same perspective is evident in Chrysostom's comments on Heb. 4:15, one of the strongest statements of Christ's identification with the human race in the New Testament: "For we have not a high priest who is unable to sympathize with our weaknesses, but one who in every respect has been tempted as we are, yet without sinning." Chrysostom sees the temptation and suffering as real experiences, but attributable to the οἰκονομία as distinguished from divine nature.

---

[283] *De Incomprehensibili* 7, 6 (PG 48, 765). He also attributes the dread of suffering to the economy in a text examined in the last chapter: "Lest they might assert that he was altogether free from human pain and so found it easy to accept death, and that he gave us encouragement without himself being in any danger of death, he showed that, even though he dreaded death, he did not refuse to undergo it, because of its efficacy for our salvation. And this is of the economy, not of the divinity" (*Hom. in Jn.* 67, 1-2 [PG 59, 371]).

"For," he says, "in that he hath suffered himself being tempted, he is able to succor them that are tempted." This is altogether low and mean, and unworthy of God. "For in that he hath suffered himself," he says. It is of him who was made flesh [περὶ τοῦ σαρκωθέντος] that he here speaks, and it was said for the full assurance of the hearers, and on account of their weakness. That is (he would say) he went through the very experience of the things which we have suffered. "Now" he is not ignorant of our sufferings; not only does he know them as God, but as man also he has known them, by the trial wherewith he was tried. He suffered much; he knows how to sympathize. And yet God is incapable of suffering; but he describes here what belongs to the flesh [τὰ τῆς σαρκώσεως], as if he had said, "even the very flesh of Christ suffered many terrible things." He knows what tribulation is not less than we who have suffered, for he himself also has suffered.[284]

Not only suffering, but also temptation is a sign of the reality of the incarnation. Chrysostom sees both as experiences of fleshly existence, which is what allows him to venture to say that now Christ knows our sufferings in a way in which he did not previously. This new knowledge is really new experience, not that God has suffered, but that he has taken a human form that suffered in as real a sense as any human being.[285]

The second type of expression that causes Chrysostom to use distinguishing terminology is that of change. The problem, of course, is to maintain the immutability of the divine nature of Christ while taking seriously the biblical expressions that under any normal interpretation would suggest a change of status or

---

[284] *Hom. in Heb.* 5, 2 (PG 63, 47-48).

[285] Note Frances Young's comment on Chrysostom's interpretation: "It is not merely that knowledge acquired by experience is more reliable and therefore essential for his work as a sympathetic High Priest, but that the reality of his experience is essential for his victory over evil to be relevant to men" ("Christological Ideas in the Greek Commentaries on the Epistle to the Hebrews," *J Th St* NS 20 [1969]: 156). In this Young sees a strong contrast with the approach of the Alexandrians who distinctly downplay this sympathetic experience. But it should be pointed out that Chrysostom does not explicitly say that this experience of suffering is the primary way salvation is obtained for the race.

even existence. If Chrysostom faced in the gospels the problem of the incarnational experience of Christ, then in the book of Hebrews he continually confronts the problem of incarnational theology. He preached thirty-four sermons on Hebrews, probably late in his career from his Constantinople seat, and they reveal the way this fourth-century preacher came to terms with the unique expressions of Hebrews concerning how Christ came into the world and his mediatorial status that resulted.

The very first verse of Hebrews raises the problem: how can it be said of the eternal Son that he was "appointed heir"? And then there is the expression "being made better than angels." Such statements apply only to the οἰκονομία, or Christ according to the flesh.

> What is "whom He appointed heir of all"? He speaks here of the flesh [the human nature]. . . . That is to say, he has made him Lord of all, which Peter also said in the Acts, "God has made him both Lord and Christ." But he has used the name "heir," declaring two things: his proper sonship [τὸ τῆς υἱότητος γνήσιον] and his indefeasible sovereignty [τὸ τῆς κυριότητος ἀναπόσπαστον].[286]

Likewise, Christ's inheritance of being made better than the angels refers to the flesh.

> Henceforward then he treats here of that which is according to the flesh [περὶ τῆς κατὰ σάρκα οἰκονομίας], since the phrase "being made better" does not express his essence according to the Spirit [οὐσίας. . . κατὰ πνεῦμα],[287] (for that was not "made" but "begotten,") but according to the flesh: for this was "made." Nevertheless the discourse here is not about being called into existence [οὐσιώσεως]. . . . Do you see that he is speaking of that which is according to the flesh? For this Name [Son], God the Word ever had; He did not afterwards "obtain it by inheritance"; nor did He afterwards become "better than the

---

[286] *Hom. in Heb.* 1, 1 (PG 63, 15). "Proper sonship" indicates the eternal quality of Christ's sonship. Cf. Eusebius of Caesarea: "the true and only-begotten child of God" [τὸν τοῦ θεοῦ παῖδα γνήσιον καὶ μονογενῆ] (*Hist. eccl.* 1, 2, 3).

[287] Κατὰ πνεῦμα according to Field's text, while others have κατὰ πατέρα.

angels, when He had purged our sins"; but he was always "better," and better without all comparison. For this is spoken according to the flesh. So truly it is our way also, when we talk of man, to speak things both high and low. Thus, when we say, "Man is nothing," "man is earth," "man is ashes," we call the whole by the worse part. But when we say, "man is an immortal animal," and "man is rational, and of kin to those on high": we call again the whole by the better part. So also in the case of Christ, sometimes Paul discourses from the less and sometimes from the better; wishing both to establish the economy, and also to teach about the incorruptible nature [ἀκρηράτου. . . φύσεως].[288]

Thus by a simple distinction between the event of incarnation and eternal existence (οὐσιώσεως) Chrysostom keeps the essential nature of the Son untouched by any process of change. Again the distinction is between the "economy" and "the incorruptible nature," or, between the essence "according to the flesh" and that "according to the Spirit." The identification of the divine nature of the Son with the Spirit is not an uncommon feature of fourth-century Greek theology.[289]

Hebrews 1:5-6 uses the phrases "thou art my Son, this day have I begotten thee" (Ps. 2:7) and "when he brings the first-begotten into the world," both phrases which speak of the Son in temporal terms. A distinction between the eternal nature of the Son and his incarnate nature is what solves the problem of the "today" of the first phrase.

> For these things indeed are spoken with reference also to the flesh: "I will be to Him a Father, and he shall be to me a son"—while this, "thou art my son, this day have I begotten thee," expresses nothing else than "from [the time] that God is."[290]

---

[288] *Hom. in Heb.* 1, 2 (PG 63, 46).

[289] See B. Bobrinsky, "The Indwelling of the Spirit in Christ: 'Pneumatic Christology' in the Cappadocian Fathers," *St. Vladimir's Theological Quarterly* 28 (1984): 49-65.

[290] *Hom. in Heb.* 2, 3 (PG 63, 24-25).

The "bringing in" of the Son is also explained by this distinction: "he said not these things concerning God the Word, but concerning that which is according to the flesh."[291]

One final example of seeming mutability in the book of Hebrews which Chrysostom discusses is the ascribing of glory to the Son. For the Son to be crowned with glory and honor[292] seems to put the Son in an inferior position vis-à-vis the Father, but Chrysostom attributes the expression specifically to Christ according to the flesh:

> Now although these things were spoken of human nature generally, they would nevertheless apply more properly to Christ according to the flesh. . . . When I say he was glorified, do not suppose that there was an accession of glory to him, for that which is of nature he always had, and received nothing in addition [ἐκείνην γὰρ τὴν τῆς φύσεως, εἶχεν ἀεὶ, οὐδὲν προσλαβών].[293]

Glorification, then, is an attribute of the incarnate nature. And the subsidiary status of that nature is made clear by Chrysostom's emphasis on the eternal nature. Full deity is the real nature of the Son.

Finally, a third type of passage which necessitates a distinguishing of natures is that which places Christ in a mediatorial role. Here again the book of Hebrews requires more explanation than other New Testament books because of its comparison of Christ with the priestly roles and rites of the Old Testament. Chrysostom states categorically that if Christ is depicted as high priest, that "is not of nature [φύσεως], but of grace [χάριτος] and condescension [συγκαταβάσεως], and humiliation [κενώσεως]."[294] The point is made even stronger in reference to Heb. 3:1-2 "consider Jesus, the apostle and high priest

---

[291] *Hom. in Heb.* 3, 1 (PG 63, 27).

[292] Heb. 2:7 from Ps. 8:5 "Thou hast crowned him with glory and honor."

[293] *Hom. in Heb.* 4, 2 (PG 63, 38); ibid. 4, 3 (PG 63, 40).

[294] *Hom. in Heb.* 7, 2 (PG 63, 63).

of our confession. He was faithful to him who appointed him, just as Moses also was faithful. . . ." Chrysostom responds:

> Therefore he [Paul] begins from the flesh, and goes up to the Godhead, where there was no longer any comparison. He began from the flesh by assuming for a time the equality, and says, "as also Moses in all his house". . . . "Who was faithful," he says, "to him that made him"—made [him] what? "Apostle and high priest." He is not speaking at all in this place of his essence [περὶ οὐσίας], nor of his Godhead [θεότητος], but so far concerning human dignities [περὶ ἀξιωμάτων ἀνθρωπίνων].[295]

The roles of apostle and high priest are thus analogous to Christ's special incarnate state, not his divine nature which, properly speaking, is his οὐσία. It is the nature of the comparison that causes Chrysostom to limit its application. The humanity of the high priest and Moses and Melchizedek, their distance from divine nature, of necessity require that these must be roles relating to the peculiar nature of the incarnation. It would be tautological to say of the divine Christ "it was fitting that we should have such a high priest, holy, blameless, unstained, separated from sinners" (Heb. 7:26) quite simply because God is in no sense capable of defilement. Such statements are made "entirely with reference to the manhood [περὶ τῆς ἀνθρωπότητος]."[296]

In commenting on Heb. 7:26 "he always lives to make intercession," Chrysostom further explains that it is the intercessory character of the work of the high priest that requires that this role pertain to Christ's incarnate and not his divine nature.

---

[295] *Hom. in Heb.* 5, 2 (PG 63, 49).

[296] *Hom. in Heb.* 13, 3 (PG 63, 106). Athanasius similarly associates such passages in Hebrews with "the economy" and not the "essence" of the Son: "Not then as wishing to signify the essence of the Word nor his natural generation from the Father, does the apostle say, 'who was faithful to him who made him'" (*Contra Arianos* 2, 7). And, "wherefore Paul was writing concerning the Word's human economy when he said, 'who was faithful to him who made him,' and not concerning his essence" (*Contra Arianos* 2, 9).

You see that he says this in respect of that which is according to the flesh. For when he [appears] as priest, then he also intercedes.... Do you see the humiliation? Do you see the manhood? For he says not that he obtained this by making intercession once for all, but continually.... Does he then always need to pray? How can this be reasonable?.... Why then is he throned with [the Father]? You see that it is a condescension.... He cannot live always, for he does live always.[297]

And Christ's intercession is temporary, a further indication that it pertains to the economy.

Do not then, having heard that he is a priest, suppose that he is always executing the priest's office. For he executed it once, and thenceforward "sat down." Lest you suppose that he is standing on high, and is a minister, he shows that the matter is an economy. For as he became a servant, so also he became a priest and a minister. But as after becoming a servant, he did not continue a servant, so also, having become a minister, he did not continue a minister.[298]

To summarize what we have established thus far: Chrysostom, like every orthodox fourth-century Greek theologian, focuses on the incarnation of Christ as the foundation of salvation although its paradoxes put every imaginable strain on common metaphysical presuppositions. The necessity of the immutability of divine nature pulls in the opposite direction of the necessity for a genuine incarnation. Chrysostom seeks, somewhere between the excesses of the docetists and those of the subordinationists, an understanding of the incarnation that preserves the confession of real divinity and real humanity in the incarnate Christ. He finds at least part of the solution in the utter uniqueness of this οἰκονομία of God. It represents a special condition of divine nature that is without comparison either by human analogy or with any other

---

[297] *Hom. in Heb.* 13, 3 (PG 63, 106).

[298] *Hom. in Heb.* 13, 3 (PG 63, 106-07).

aspect of the life and being of God. There is no point at which the divine Logos is not the only determinative subject of the actions of Christ; nevertheless, biblical language does at times focus on the special characteristics of the incarnate state of Christ—the οἰκονομία, or the "humanity," or simply, the "flesh." Biblical language implies real distinctions, in other words, but not distinctions that exclude the necessary ἕνωσις of divinity and humanity, mysterious though that may be. Where distinctions must be made is where language is encountered that speaks of human identification, change, or mediation.

Chrysostom does more, however, than simply identify verses of Scripture according to the scheme "as God—as man." His explanation of how the divine Word maintained his divinity while enfleshed is most often an appeal to understanding the incarnation as condescension.

## The Incarnation as Condescension

K. Duchatelez observes: "Parmi les réalités très riches qui commandent toute l'histoire du salut et auxquelles l'antiquité chrétienne était particulièrement sensible, figure la *sugkatabasis*, la «condescendance»."[299] Συγκατάβασις was for many of the Greek Fathers from the time of Origen on a convenient term to use with reference to those acts of God in which he directly deals with elements of the creation. Divine immanence was always a problem for Greek theology, especially in its witness to its surrounding Greek pagan culture. Christians reasoned that certain extraordinary events are to be explained on the basis of the grace of God by which he voluntarily manifests himself to his creation through a condescension of his own nature. Such events may include theophanies, the inspiration of the Scriptures, and other revelatory actions, but most especially it is represented in the incarnation of Christ.

---

[299] K. Duchatelez, "La «condescendance» divine et l'histoire du salut," *Nouvelle Revue Theologique* 95 (1973): 593.

Condescension is undoubtably one of Chrysostom's favorite theological themes. According to H. Pinard, "Il revient si fréquemment sur cette idée et il lui donne un tel relief, qu'on peut en quelque sorte le nommer 'le docteur de la condescendance.'"[300] The concept is basic to his understanding of revelation in general and thus serves as a key to the mysteries of biblical inspiration. For a preacher like Chrysostom who systematically treats biblical texts in his homilies, the concept of condescension is particularly helpful in explaining difficult, often anthropomorphic passages. With regard to the incarnation, it is a way of explaining many of the most humble descriptions of Christ, for example his seeming ignorance or inability to carry out certain actions. Several key questions arise as a consequence: does the condescension occur at an ontological level? If not—and this is Chrysostom's position— then how is the incarnation anything more than docetic? How does condescension relate to kenosis? And finally, does this condescension further define the relationship of the divine and the human in Christ?

## The Meaning of Συγκατάβασις

In his survey of the use of συγκατάβασις in the Greek Fathers from Origen on, Duchatelez describes the development of the term from its simplest sense "to descend together with," or "at the same time as," to its further connotation of descending to an inferior, both readily found in Greek literature. The next logical step is condescension as accomodation or adaptation to the level or capacity of an inferior. Here Christians found a highly useful description of God's activities in the worldly realm.[301]

---

[300] H. Pinard, "Les infiltrations païennes dans l'Ancienne Loi d'apres les Pères de l'Eglise. La thèse de la condescendance," *Recherches des science religieuse* 9 (1919): 209.

[301] "Les Pères de l'Eglise, eux, usent abondamment de cette terminologie pour exalter la manière dont Dieu et le Christ, dans l'économie du salut, adaptent leur manière d'agir et de parler" (Duchatelez, "La «condescendance»," p. 598).

The Greek Fathers from Origen on utilized the concept on two different levels—apologetics and theology. Duchatelez says of Origen's apologetic use of it, "Ses considérations sont élaborées pour une part en vue d'objets difficilement acceptables pour des esprits de culture grecque, et injustifiables, en particulier, aux yeux du philosophe païen Celse, à savoir une initiative de Dieu intervenant directement dans l'histoire pour améliorer la situation morale des hommes, et surtout le fait même de l'Incarnation."[302] Συγκατάβασις describes the way the transcendent God has involved himself in human affairs without thereby being corrupted in the process. More importantly, condescension is for man's sake, because human nature is entirely incapable of perceiving the divine nature. Origen says of the Logos:

> On the contrary, because of his exceeding love towards man he was able to give the educated a conception of God which could raise their soul from earthly things, and nevertheless came down to the level even of the more defective capacities of ordinary men and simple women and slaves, and, in general, of people who have been helped by none but by Jesus alone to live a better life, so far as they can, and to accept doctrines about God such as they had the capacity to receive.[303]

Συγκατάβασις has further apologetic value for the Fathers in their attempts to explain to their pagan challengers the necessity for and the peculiarities of salvation history. That salvation would come through a historical process was problematic enough, but what further complicated the picture was a two-fold covenant with widely divergent conditions and forms. Why would God have used a particular people—the Jews—in what was intended as a universal redemption? And why would God sanction the legalisms of the Jews including something as base as animal sacrifice, a practice seemingly more linked to ignorant pagan rites than to an intellectually satisfying faith? Finally, why would God then withdraw his approval for something that he himself had

---

[302] Ibid., p. 598.

[303] *Contra Celsum* 7, 41, tr. by Henry Chadwick (Cambridge, 1965), p. 429.

instituted? The explanation provided by several of the Fathers, but none more so than Chrysostom, is that salvation history is to be interpreted as a grand scheme of divine condescension.[304]

Stephen Benin has recently made a comparison of Augustine and Chrysostom on this point. Both were highly educated and thus tended to relate salvation history to a divine process of education.

> Augustine and Chrysostom appreciated the power and influence of teachers and of pedagogical techniques. Both viewed God as the teacher, and both were captivated by the divine method of instruction. They saw this method as one of divine accommodation; that is, the Lord adapted his lessons and plan to human capacities. . . . It helped them interpret scripture, it aided them in defending the faith and in confounding schismatics, and it enhanced their understanding of history and of the implementation of the divine plan within the historical process, especially in the age of Christ.[305]

Benin goes on to point out that condescension or accommodation is naturally harmonious with the Platonic world-view reflected in so many of the Fathers. Manifestations of condescension like the Jewish cult are signs and symbols of greater, spiritual realities.[306] It follows also that condescension is

---

[304] H. Pinard demonstrates how, from the earliest Jewish-Christian dialogues of Justin Martyr on, condescension was one way of explaining the relationship between the religious rites and principles of pagans, Jews, and Christians. The Fathers "ont regardé presque tous le rituel compliqué de l'Ancienne Loi comme une concession aux tendances paganisantes d'une nation corrompue par son séjour prolongé au milieu des idolâtres et par le contact incessant de peuples polythéistes. Ils ont pris soin toutefois de faire remarquer que Jahvé, en recevant certains rites de style païen, avait épuré la morale qui les accompagnait ailleurs, transformé les dogmes qui les inspiraient et combiné la législation juive, de manière à ce qu'elle fût comme un mur protecteur entre les Hébreux et les Gentils, assurât le triomphe du monothéisme et préparât l'économie plus parfaite du Nouveau Testament" ("Les infiltrations païennes," p. 216).

[305] Stephen D. Benin, "Sacrifice as Education in Augustine and Chrysostom," *Church History* 52 (1983): 7.

[306] Ibid., p.19.

more consistent with an allegorical exegesis. Thus, it is not accurate to picture Chrysostom exclusively as a representative of an Antiochene exegetical school that is completely historical and Aristotelian in approach.[307]

What emerges in Augustine and Chrysostom is a comprehensive scheme of salvation history. Condescension is the way it has been and is unfolding. God uses the trappings of history and of the material world to reveal himself and his intentions, but behind it all is a divine nature oblivious to passion and mutability. Thus,

> ... for Chrysostom the accommodation was much more than a powerful hermeneutical device and a way of explaining away customs which hinted at an anthropomorphic deity. In Chryso- stom's hands divine accomodation became nothing less than the very process of divine communication, divine revelation, and divine salvation. It was the essence of the divine, grand cosmic plan.[308]

The employment of condescension thus goes beyond apologetic concern. It becomes both a broad hermeneutical principle and a standard theological category.

Chrysostom's most complete definition of condescension occurs not in reference to the incarnation, but in a discussion of the incomprehensibility of the divine nature. In arguing against the Anomoeans' assertion that they could identify the essence of God, Chrysostom points out that not even angels can know it. At best, they view a condescension of the divine nature which itself requires a veiling of its glory. Such is the point of the covering of the eyes of the seraphim of Isaiah's vision.

---

[307] Benin corrects this frequently held assumption, as, for instance represented in H. Oberman who says that Chrysostom completely rejected allegory (*Forerunners of the Reformation* [Philadelphia, 1981], p. 282). "Chrysostom's use of accommodation disproves Oberman's assertion, which is the normal way of describing Chrysostom in particular and the Antiochene school in general. Chrysostom's use of accommodation should prove that one must not categorize any patristic school too rigidly" (Ibid., p. 20, note 70).

[308] Ibid., p. 18.

Yet they did not see the pure light itself nor the pure essence itself. What they saw was a condescension accommodated to their nature. What is this condescension? God condescends whenever he is not seen as he is, but in the way one incapable of beholding him is able to look upon him. In this way God reveals himself by accommodating what he reveals to the weakness of vision of those who behold him. And it is clear from Isaiah's very words that, in his case, he saw God by such condescension, for he said: "I saw the Lord sitting on a high and lofty throne." But God is not sitting. This is a posture for bodily beings. And Isaiah said: "On a throne." But God is not encompassed or enclosed by a throne; divinity cannot be circumscribed by limits. Nonetheless, the Seraphim could not endure God's condescension even though they were only standing near.[309]

The meaning of condescension, then, is this: because of the vast difference between divine nature and all created natures, God's contact with the created realm necessarily involves forms of revelation symbolic of the essential reality of the divine nature about which they communicate. In Chrysostom's words, "God condescends whenever he is not seen as he is, but in the way one incapable of beholding him is able to look upon him," that is, at best, the divine nature is revealed by accommodation. The importance of this in understanding Chrysostom's Christology will become apparent when we come to texts in which condescension is applied to the human manifestation of Christ.

Finally, we must note the close relationship between condescension and revelation. F. H. Chase in his study of

---

[309] *De Incomprehensibili* 3, 160-73 (Malingrey, p. 200). So also the angels in heaven do not pretend to be able to perceive God's essence, which is more than can be said of the Anomoeans: "Do you think that the angels in heaven talk over and ask each other questions about the divine essence? By no means! What are the angels doing? They give glory to God, they adore him, they chant without ceasing. . . . 'Holy, holy, holy,' and they turn away their eyes because they cannot endure God's presence as he comes down to adapt himself to them in condescension. . . . The angels in heaven give him glory; these heretics on earth carry on meddlesome investigations" (*De Incomprehensibili* 1, 308-23 [Malingrey pp. 126f.]).

Chrysostom's exegesis describes συγκατάβασις as a central hermeneutical principle.[310] Many details of the Old Testament are explained on the basis of the accommodation inherent in the act of revelation: man's likeness to God (Gen. 1:26) is not a physical likeness, nor is God's breathing into man the breath of life a transference of the essence of God—both expressions are not what they seem to be. So also, many of the commands of the Law are condescensions in the sense of being part of a necessary but impermanent educational process. And all theophanies of the Old Testament fit into the category of condescension, a particularly important point when Chrysostom defends the incomprehensibility of the divine nature.[311]

The problem of relativity in revelation arises when both the form and the substance of revelation are modified by condescension. The balancing principle that Chrysostom employs is that of ἀκρίβεια—the accuracy and precision of the Scriptures. Even when the Scriptures contain statements that are not literally true, they are none the less analogously true, in the same way that a teacher says true things in the way children would speak.

> A teacher who is full of wisdom stammers along with his stammering young students. But the teacher's stammering does

---

[310] F. H. Chase, *Chrysostom: a Study in the History of Biblical Interpretation* (Cambridge, 1887), pp. 41-49. Chase notes the logical link between the doctrines of revelation and incarnation: "The great principle expressed by the word συγκατάβασις is of deep and wide application. As in the historical incarnation the Eternal Word became flesh, so in the Bible the glory of God veils itself in the fleshly garment of human thought and language" (p. 42).

[311] Jn. 1:18, "No one has ever seen God," is the pivotal text in this defense, but the problem of numerous theophanies remains. Chrysostom gathers together several such references (Isa. 6:1 "I saw the Lord. . ."; Amos 9:1 "I saw the Lord. . ."; etc.) and then comments: "All the cases cited were instances of God's condescension and accommodation. That no one of those prophets saw God's essence in its pure state is clear from the fact that each one saw him in a different way. . . . They cannot endure to comprehend him with a pure and perfect knowledge; they dare not look fixedly at his essence pure and entire; they dare not look at him even after he has accommodated himself to them" (*De Incomprehensibili* 4, 183-85; 228-33 [Malingrey, pp. 244; 246]).

not come from a lack of learning; it is a sign of the concern he feels toward the children. In the same way, Christ did not do these things [i.e. pray, wash his disciples' feet] because of the lowliness of his essence [οὐ δί εὐτέλειαν τῆς οὐσίας]. He did them because he was condescending to us.[312]

## Condescension in the Incarnation

Before considering the numerous ways in which Chrysostom interprets the particular words and activities of the incarnate Christ as condescension and the reasons for it, we should first note that Chrysostom identifies the whole of the incarnation itself as a grand condescension. In the sixth homily against the Anomoeans, preached just days before Christmas, Chrysostom tells his congregation that the nativity provides more reason for fear and trembling than all the other feasts:

> Even though he was free from any sin, he did take upon himself a mortal body, and that should make us marvel. That he who is God was willing to become man, that he endured to accommodate himself to our weakness and to come down to our level is too great for our minds to grasp. It makes us shudder with the deepest holy fear; it fills us with terror and trembling.[313]

The incarnate life of Christ is a συγκατάβασις in which is contained the important testimony of the divine οἰκονομία. The condescension carried out in the incarnation of the Son does not, nevertheless, affect his divine nature.

> He made his defense neither as man alone, nor as God alone, but now as one, again as the other. He wished the two truths to be believed: both the condescension of the incarnation and the dignity of his godhead [καὶ τῆς οἰκονομίας τὴν συγκατάβασιν, καὶ τῆς θεότητος τὸ ἀξίωμα].[314]

---

[312] *De Incomprehensibili* 10, 2 (PG 48, 786).

[313] *De Incomprehensibili* 6, 4 (PG 48, 753).

[314] *Hom. in Jn.* 38, 3 (PG 59, 214).

In one sense, then, just as οἰκονομία often serves as a synonym for the incarnate life of Christ or his physical flesh (and so, the opposite of the divine nature), so also can συγκατάβασις.

More often, however, condescension is used in a dynamic sense—it is the way divine nature could take human form and yet not involve change or degeneration. Thus Chrysostom explains the emptying of Phil. 2 as a change of status which did not thereby lessen the glory of the Son:

> With full confidence he took on himself the nature and form of a servant. He knew full well that condescension and accomodation in no way could lessen his glory.[315]

In other words, it is the fact that συγκατάβασις is one step removed from reality that the incarnate life of Christ does not contradict his eternal divine nature. We are reminded of Chrysostom's own definition of condescension: "God condescends whenever he is not seen as he is." Chrysostom often explains events and sayings in the gospels as things that seem to be what they are not.

Where Chrysostom guards himself from simple docetism is his strong affirmation of the true flesh of Christ. This is not condescension.

> Angels often appeared on earth in the form of man, as did God himself. But their appearances were not in true flesh but by a condescension. To prevent you from thinking that his coming to earth was as those others were, and to give you solid grounds for truly believing that his was real flesh, he was conceived, born, and nurtured.[316]

---

[315] *De Incomprehensibili* 10, 5 (PG 48, 793).

[316] *De Incomprehensibili* 7, 6 (PG 48, 765). It is interesting that Chrysostom has quite a different opinion about the resurrection body of Christ. The marks of the nails and Jesus' eating with his disciples are not signs of a genuine flesh but a condescension: "One might understandably be puzzled as to how an incorruptible body could show marks of the nails and be capable of being touched by a mortal hand. However, do not be disturbed, for the phenomenon was an evidence of Christ's condescension.... Christ made his appearance as he did so that the resurrection would be believed and so that they would know that it was he—the

Elsewhere Chrysostom does use συγκατάβασις in reference to the flesh of Christ, but only in the sense of the humility which typified the incarnation.

We will now consider some of the specific applications of συγκατάβασις in the exegesis of Chrysostom. The majority of his references to condescension in the incarnate Christ occur when he encounters biblical texts (or is made to do so by Neo-Arians) which are problematic for the divine nature of the Son. One such category of texts includes those which describe a relationship of dependence or submission between the Son and the Father. Condescension is the way to explain Jesus' statements that he was sent by the Father,[317] that he could do nothing apart from the will of the Father,[318] that the Father loved him because he laid down his life,[319] that he was going to the Father,[320] or that the Father gave disciples[321] or glory[322] to the Son. No such statement, Chrysostom reminds his congregations, should be taken at its surface meaning.

---

very one who had been crucified—and not someone else who had arisen instead of him." In Chrysostom's mind the consubstantiality of the human flesh of Christ and that of human beings does not apply to the resurrection body, an indication of the degree of change he assumes takes place in the resurrection itself.

[317] "Now, being 'sent' implies change in place and God is everywhere present. . . . Do you see that in this text he once again displayed much condescension in his words?" (*Hom. in Jn.* 39, 2 [PG 59, 222]).

[318] Christ was saying that he was doing nothing contrary to the Father's will. *Hom. in Jn.* 39, 4 (PG 59, 225).

[319] "What, then, was he without the Father's love before that? Did the Father now begin to love him, and did we actually become the cause of his love for him? Do you see how much he condescended to our lowliness?" (*Hom. in Jn.* 60, 2 [PG 59, 330]).

[320] *Hom. in Jn.* 74, 2 (PG 59, 402).

[321] "Hence, the words, 'thou has given' were used only for the sake of condescending to the weakness of his listeners. For the things that the Father has are the Son's and the things that the Son has are the Father's. Now, this cannot be said of the Son merely as man, but only insofar as he is greater" (*Hom. in Jn.* 81, 1 [PG 59, 439]).

[322] *Hom. in Jn.* 82, 2 (PG 59, 445).

A second type of statement that should be attributed to condescension is that which seems to imply a need—other than physical—which Christ had. Most often this comes up with reference to Christ's prayers. Chrysostom firmly explains at every such instance that Christ did not have to pray, but did so as a condescension that would provide an example. He did not have to pray before doing a miracle,[323] and he did not have to give thanks before receiving food, even though in both cases he did.[324] Chrysostom often alludes to the raising of Lazarus which evidently was much used by the Neo-Arians.[325] Christ would not have had to come to the tomb in order to raise Lazarus, and he did not have to pray.[326] If Jesus could do something as lowly as wash the feet of Judas, it should not be difficult to imagine that he would pray publicly "because of the weakness of the Jews."[327]

At one point in the important seventh homily against the Anomoeans Chrysostom provides a summary of reasons why lowly things are said about Christ in the Scriptures. (1) The true flesh of Christ involves him in a true humility:

> The first reason is also the most important, namely, that he was clothed with flesh [τὸ σάρκα αὐτὸν περιβεβλῆσθαι] and he wished all men, both of those days and of later ages, to believe that what they saw was not simply a shadow or an apparent form but a true nature [ἀλήθεια φύσεως].[328]

---

[323] "It is very clear that he prayed before this miracle in condescension to our lowliness" (*Hom. in Jn.* 42, 2 [PG 59, 242]).

[324] *Hom. in Jn.* 43, 1 (PG 59, 246).

[325] "For many of the heretics are saying that the Son is not like the Father. Why? Because, they say, Christ had need of prayer to raise Lazarus back to life; if he had not prayed, he would not have brought him back from the dead" (*De Incomprehensibili* 9, 1 [PG 48, 779]).

[326] Especially problematic is Jesus' statement: "Father, I thank you that you heard me" (John 11:41). These words are, explains Chrysostom, "an exaggeration," stemming "not from his true dignity, but from his condescension" (*Hom. in Jn.* 64, 3 [PG 59, 358]).

[327] *De Incomprehensibili* 9, 1 (PG 48, 780).

[328] *De Incomprehensibili* 7, 3 (PG 48, 759).

(2) The "weakness" of those to whom Christ revealed himself required a pedagogical bridge. Otherwise, the message would have been rejected out of hand because human perception is only able to receive a veiled version of the divine nature.[329] (3) Speaking out of condescension was the best way for Christ to teach humility to his disciples. (4) Lowly statements by and about Christ made it clear—against Sabellians—that there are three persons in the godhead. (5) These statements also prove that Christ is not himself "the first and unbegotten substance... greater than the Father who had begotten him." And finally, (6) statements of humility refuted the suspicion and ill will of the Jews.

Condescension is thus a key to interpreting christological passages in Chrysostom. He uses it to describe a mode by which the divine Christ takes human roles for two main reasons: either to provide a revelation of deity in veiled form because of human inability to look upon pure deity; or to provide a model of human behavior. In either case, the human functions of Christ are not detached from the divine will of the Logos, but have their genesis in the οἰκονομία of condescension. On the other hand, the human flesh of Christ is a material reality distinct from the divine nature. His real humanity consists primarily in his real flesh, and its attendant physical needs and physical suffering. Condescension when applied to the flesh is used in the sense of voluntary humility, not in the sense of accommodation.

---

[329] "If ever he were to have said anything beyond the grasp of human nature, the men who heard him would be upset and scandalized. But if he ever were to say something in a lowly and human fashion, they would run to him and accept what he said." Chrysostom uses as evidence the simple rejection that resulted from such lofty statements as "Before Abraham came to be, I am," "I am the bread of life," and others. We may note the frequency with which Chrysostom appeals to this point. "I now declare and will keep repeating something that I have often said. And what is this? That when Jesus is at the point of arriving at teachings that are sublime he frequently restrains himself in consideration of the weakness of his hearers, and does not dwell for long on subjects befitting his greatness, but rather on those which condescend to their lowliness" (*Hom. in Jn.* 27, 1 [PG 59, 157]).

## The Way of Salvation—Moral Accomplishment and Divinization

Insofar as soteriology and Christology are interconnected, it will be helpful to note some of the major soteriological emphases brought out in Chrysostom's exegesis and his occasional treatises. One common observation made in the analysis of Antiochene and Alexandrian schools, is the fundamentally different soteriologies they represent. The Antiochenes are said to be much more humanistic and Aristotelian in their understanding of salvation. The way of salvation is that of moral accomplishment, and the corresponding Christology sees Jesus as the exemplar and teacher who provides his followers a righteousness based on imitation. Consequently, the full humanity of Christ, including intellectual and volitional integrity, is crucial because it demonstrates the real possibility of moral accomplishment on the human level. On the other hand, the Alexandrian approach, it is said, pictures salvation in more cosmic and mystical terms, indicative of Platonic assumptions. A divinization of humanity occurs in the incarnation itself as divine and human natures are united and the process of corruption in human nature is reversed. In this understanding the element of moral accomplishment in the God-man is unnecessary. As Frances Young puts it: "In contrast to Cyril's dominant interest in the conquest of human weakness by the power of God, the Antiochene commentators concentrate on the exemplary value of the Saviour's own conquest of human weakness, temptation, and suffering."[330] If in the first view the

---

[330] Frances Young, "Christological Ideas in the Greek Commentaries on the Epistle to the Hebrews," *J Th St* NS 20 (1969): 155. Young notes elsewhere that "the classic studes of Chrysostom invariably enquire how far his thought was Pelagian; but surely that is an unjustifiable question. The paradox of divine grace and human freedom would not become a controversial issue until four years after his death. Chrysostom was well aware that in the achievement of salvation neither God's grace nor human effort was sufficient without the other. Thus he often coupled both emphases.... Augustine as well as Pelagius found passages in Chrysostom to support his case" (*From Nicaea to Chalcedon*, p.150).

incarnate life of Christ is a model of salvation, in the second it is the reality of salvation.

Chrysostom has elements of both soteriological approaches. He very definitely sees Christ as an exemplar, but also speaks in terms of the elevation of human nature through Christ's incarnation.

## An Ethical Approach to Salvation

The fact that Chrysostom, especially in his preaching on the gospels and Hebrews, finds many occasions to point to the activities of Christ as examples for virtuous living probably does not in itself mean that Chrysostom had a completely moralistic view of salvation. The homily, by its very nature, leads to a moral exhortation, and if the text at hand provides anything that can be turned into an ethical application, the preacher will use it in that way. So it is not surprising that Christ is the model for gentleness, patience, and meekness in his humiliation at the hands of Pilate,[331] or an example of humility in the way he often set aside his sovereign prerogatives.[332] In that he prayed, he was providing a conscious demonstration of what should be normative in the lives of his followers,[333] and his willingness to die is the example for all Christian self-sacrifice.

---

[331] *Hom. in Jn.* 83, 5 (PG 59, 453). Similarly, Jesus' general reaction to his enemies teaches meekness: "He remained silent. . . . also to teach us to be gentle and patient in all circumstances. Let us, then, imitate him" (*Hom. in Jn.* 60, 3-4 [PG 59, 332]).

[332] E.g., Jesus refused to be made king by the Jews "to teach us to despise worldly honors and to show that he was in need of nothing belonging to earth. He who had chosen for himself everything lowly—mother, home, city, rearing, and clothing—was not going to make a display of himself afterwards by worldly means" (*Hom. in Jn.* 42, 3 [PG 59, 243]).

[333] "For what purpose does he go up into the mountain? To teach us, that loneliness and retirement is good, when we are to pray to God. . . . there [he] often spends the whole night in prayer, teaching us earnestly to seek such quietness in our prayers, as the time and place may confer" (*Hom. in Matt.* 50, 1 (PG 58, 503]).

Chrysostom identifies the principle behind such demonstrations when discussing Jesus' going to the feast in Jerusalem secretly so as to avoid his enemies:

> The actions performed by Christ in a human way were so performed not merely for the purpose of confirming the incarnation [τὰ ἀνθρωπίνως ὑπὸ τοῦ Χριστοῦ οἰκονομούμενα, οὐ διὰ τοῦτο μόνον οἰκονομεῖται], but also that he might instruct us to virtuous living. For, if he did everything as God, whence would we be able to learn what we ought to do when faced with trials outside the realm of our experience?[334]

Many such actions, then, are forms of condescension in that they do not reflect the reality of Christ's experience, but rather, his didactic intentions.[335]

More than moral lessons, however, these demonstrations reflect the basic significance of the whole of the incarnation: in the condescension of the incarnation are the means, the form, and the consequences of salvation. Chrysostom comments on Jn. 5:31-34 where Jesus qualifies the fact that he seems somewhat dependent upon the testimony of John the Baptist: "If I alone bear witness of myself, my testimony is not true. . . . But the witness which I receive is not from man; but I say these things that you may be saved":

> And so we have a correct explanation, and one worthy of God, for his speaking with humble words: namely, his condescension and his teaching us to act with moderation; also, the salvation he planned to come to us by this means [τὴν διὰ ταύτης ἡμῖν

---

[334] Hom. in Jn. 49, 1 (PG 59, 273).

[335] Chrysostom thus often depicts Christ as the Teacher (e.g. "He has furnished us with teaching from above, from heaven, in order that he may remove our thoughts thither, that we may become imitators of our teacher according as we are able" (Hom. in Jn. 15, 3 [PG 59, 101]). Yet, "teacher" is not a totally adequate title for Christ because of his consubstantiality with the Father. Christ would not have spoken as he did "if he were merely a teacher and actually was of a different substance" (Hom. in Jn. 53, 4 [PG 59, 291]). Nicodemus used an insufficient designation for Christ when he called him a "teacher from God" (Hom. in Jn. 24, 2 [PG 59, 145]).

οἰκονομουμένην σωτηρίαν]. This he himself made clear when he said in another place: "I say these things that you may be saved."[336]

The way of salvation is not relegated merely to the realm of moral accomplishment here, but there is a clear link. Salvation is fully accomplished when the necessary condescension of the incarnation produces in the Christian an analogous personal condescension—humility in moral terms. Of all the virtues, humility is the one Chrysostom most frequently highlights. The core of the moral problem of the human race is pride, and the overwhelming humility of Christ continually demonstrates the meaning of righteousness.

A crucial concept for an ethical soteriology is the possibility of temptation in Jesus. For Theodore of Mopsuetia, for instance, the reality of temptation is a necessary aspect of the incarnation, otherwise Christ could not have accomplished a genuine victory over it and there would be no objective ethical basis for salvation. Cyril, on the other hand, could never entertain the possibility of real temptation because he would not allow a distinction between the manhood and the divine Logos. Chrysostom's understanding comes out in his discussion of Heb. 2:18 "because he himself has suffered and been tempted, he is able to help those who are tempted."[337] In response to this passage from Hebrews and others like it we do find Chrysostom locating such experiences in the manhood of Christ, thus showing himself more willing than Cyril

---

[336] *Hom. in Jn.* 39, 2 (PG 59, 221).

[337] "This is altogether low and mean and unworthy of God. 'For in that he has suffered himself,' he says. It is of him who was made flesh that he here speaks, and it was said for the full assurance of the hearers, and on account of their weakness. . . . 'Now' he is not ignorant of our sufferings; not only does he know them as God, but as man also he has known them, by the trial wherewith he was tried. He suffered much, he knows how to sympathize. And yet God is incapable of suffering; but he describes here what belongs to the incarnation, as if he had said, 'even the very flesh of Christ suffered many terrible things.' He knows what tribulation is. He knows what temptation is, not less than we who have suffered, for he himself has suffered" (*Hom. in Heb.* 5, 2 [PG 63, 47-48]).

to associate temptation with Christ. But once again the question must be raised whether this indicates a real psychological conflict and thus a real distinction between the Logos and a freely functioning human mind and soul. There is reason to doubt that this is Chrysostom's emphasis because, as we have seen before, he explicitly locates the experience in the flesh of Christ.[338] As such, the conquest over temptation is the same type of experience as the real fleshly suffering, and the man-God contrast is the familiar distinction between divine nature and corporeality.

Chrysostom, in other words, may be more willing than Cyril to speak of temptation in the incarnate life of Christ, but less inclined than Theodore to make of this temptation a point of victory by the humanity of Christ which makes subsequent human victories over sin a possibility. The middle way that Chrysostom takes is to see in the incarnate Christ a demonstration of human obedience and victory over sin. The real humanity of Christ is the necessary instrument for such a demonstration, but Chrysostom stops short of actually attributing the victory to the human nature of Christ.

## A Mystical Approach to Salvation

Salvation as divinization became a common theological theory in the East at least from the time of Origen. As J. N. D. Kelly says:

> [Origen] conceives of Jesus's human nature as having been progressively deified through its union with the Logos; after

---

[338] Chrysostom understands Heb. 4:15 which says Christ was "in all points tempted like as we are, yet without sin" to be indicating a common ground between the humanity of Christ and the human race in two respects: the external difficulties he encountered ("he was persecuted, was spit upon, was accused, was mocked at, was falsely informed against, was driven out, at last was crucified"), and the real flesh he possessed ("it was 'like' our flesh, since in nature it was the same with us, but in sin no longer the same"). What he does not say is that an inner spiritual conflict obtained in Christ's case. *Hom. in Heb.* 7, 2 (PG 63, 63).

the resurrection its materiality disappears and His human soul becomes fused ineffably with the Logos.[339]

The view, often seen against the backdrop of Platonic realism, sees humanity as a whole, and the incarnation of Christ as the universal provision for the reversal of corruption in the race. While Chrysostom employs other theories of salvation—that of propitiatory sacrifice, or ransom from the Devil—he also has some elements of this mystical approach as well.[340]

The fourth-century Greek Fathers emphasize different christological elements in this theory of restoration. Fundamentally, the incarnation itself is the redeeming act, but the resurrection or even the ascension may be significant for the recapitulation. Chrysostom usually speaks either in general terms of the uniting of human and divine natures in Christ, or of the elevation of human nature to heaven.

The foundation of salvation is already established with the birth of Christ wherein is joined "the old covenant with the new, God's nature with man's, the things that are his with ours." In God's becoming man is the possibility of men becoming sons of God, or, to put it the other way around, "he was born of a woman, so that you might cease to be the son of a woman." Thus, in the birth itself is contained "the sum of the whole οἰκονομία,"

---

[339] Kelly, *Early Christian Doctrines*, p.184. Origen writes: "With Jesus human and divine nature began to be woven together, so that by fellowship with divinity human nature might become divine, not only in Jesus Himself, but also in all those who believe and embrace the life which Jesus taught" (*Contra Celsum* 3, 28). Earlier hints are evident in Irenaeus in his theory of recapitulation. Irenaeus writes: "Because of his measureless love, He became what we are in order to enable us to become what he is" (*Haer.* 5, praef.).

[340] Chrysostom is not the only Greek author to simultaneously employ various soteriological theories. J. N. D. Kelly notes: "These various theories, however, despite appearances, should not be regarded as in fact mutually incompatible. They were all of them attempts to elucidate the same great truth from different angles; their superficial divergences are often due to the different Biblical images from which they started, and there is no logical reason why, carefully stated, they should not be regarded as complementary" (*Early Christian Doctrines*, p. 376).

the "origin and root of all our blessings."[341] The consubstantiality of Christ's humanity and ours is what determines that the union of humanity and divinity in him accrues to man's benefit: "even as some skilled architect who restores a house fallen to decay with age, so he restored our common nature."[342] And conversely, the Son's consubstantiality with the Father assures salvation: "How does he make us gods and sons, if he is not true God?"[343]

The central truth of the gospel, Chrysostom says in his introduction to the book of Matthew, is: "God on earth, man in heaven, and all become mingled together... and reconciliation made between God and our nature."[344] He maintains that though the union of natures results in the restoration of the lesser nature, the higher nature is not conversely affected:

> He became the Son of Man, though he was the Son of God, in order that he might make the sons of men children of God. In truth, to mingle the high with the low works no harm to the honor of the high, but raises the lowly up from its very humble estate.[345] Accordingly, this is also true in the case of Christ. He in no wise lowered his own nature [ἰδίαν φύσιν] by this descent, but elevated us, who had always been in a state of ignominy and darkness, to ineffable glory.[346]

---

[341] *Hom. in Matt.* 2, 3 (PG 57, 27).

[342] *Hom. in Jn.* 12, 2 (PG 59, 83).

[343] Πῶς δὲ ἡμᾶς Θεοὺς ποιεῖ καὶ υἱοὺς, τῶς ἐστι Θεός... (*Hom. in Jn.* 80, 2 [PG 59, 435]).

[344] *Hom. in Matt.* 1, 2 (PG 57, 15).

[345] Τὸ γὰρ ὑψηλὸν τῷ ταπεινῷ προσομιλοῦν, αὐτὸ μὲν οὐδὲν εἰς τὴν οἰκείαν παραβλάπτεται δόξαν· ἐκεῖνο δὲ ἀπὸ τῆς πολλῆς ἀνίστησι ταπεινότητος.

[346] *Hom. in Jn.* 11, 1 (PG 59, 79). An analogous "mingling" of natures occurs in the Eucharist which also results in the restoration of the lesser nature: "with this we are fed, and we are commingled [ἀναφυρόμεθα], and we are made one body and one flesh with Christ.... [He] feeds us with his own blood, and by all means entwines [συμπλέκει] us with himself.... He was born of our substance [ἐγεννήθη ἐκ τῆς ἡμετερας οὐσίας].... For if he came unto our nature, it is quite plain that it was to all, but if to all, then to each one.... With each one of the faithful does he mingle [ἀναμίγνυσιν] himself in the mysteries" (*Hom. in Matt.* 82, 5 [PG 58, 744]).

One other theme which indicates a mystical or realistic soteriology recurs in Chrysostom: that of the raising of human nature in the heavenly session of Christ. The significance of the Word becoming flesh and dwelling among us (Jn. 1:14) is not only that God took human form, but that thereafter he carried it with him, elevating it to heavenly status.

> He dwells always in this tabernacle, for he put on our flesh, not to put if off again, but to have it always with him. If this were not so, he would not have deemed it worthy of his royal throne, and, bearing it, would not have had it adored by all the host above.[347]

When Jesus prayed: "Father, glorify me with thyself, with the glory that I had with thee before the world existed" (Jn. 17:5), he was projecting the raising of human nature to incorruptibility and a share in the royal throne.[348] This is a primary image of salvation for Chrysostom, that of human nature itself seated on the royal throne of Christ:

> It is a great and wonderful thing, and full of amazement that our flesh should sit on high, and be adored by angels and archangels. . . . I am amazed at it, and imagine to myself great things concerning the human race. For I see that the introductions are great and splendid, and that God has great zeal on behalf of our nature.[349]

The final fruit of the condescension of the incarnation, then, is its own reversal. The exaltation of human nature is most evident in the elevation of Christ to heaven, as man. While authors like Athanasius may be content to point mainly to the incarnation itself as the recapitulation, Chrysostom sees the enfleshment of the Logos as the initial step which finds its completion when that flesh is glorified. Chrysostom's close adherence to the biblical text

---

[347] *Hom. in Jn.* 11, 2 (PG 59, 80). See also *Hom. in Matt.* 1, 1 (PG 57, 15): "Our nature has been carried up into heaven."

[348] *Hom. in Jn.* 80, 2-3 (PG 59, 435).

[349] *Hom. in Heb.* 5, 1 (PG 63, 46-47).

leads him to cast the incarnation in the language of a condescension which is descriptive of both the phenomena and the consequences of the incarnation.

## Summary

Chrysostom's understanding of the incarnation includes two different types of distinctions. The first is necessitated by salvation history—that of the divine Son before the incarnation and after it. This temporal rather than ontological distinction describes the Son κατὰ τῆς οἰκονομίας, that is, during the time of God's ultimate outpouring of grace. Unusual attributions are made of the Son only because of the extraordinary nature of the incarnate state of Christ.

The second type of distinction—that of the divine nature of the Son and his flesh—is employed to keep divinity distinct from materiality. Chrysostom is guarding the real corporeality of Christ against docetic interpretations, and, at the same time, is answering the Arians by making the flesh of Christ the subject of the sufferings.

Both distinctions are explained by the nature of the incarnation which is condescension. The setting aside of divine prerogatives and the taking of flesh is the greatest act of divine philanthropy, which in turn becomes a model for humility. And many of the "lowly" things said by or about Christ are not to be taken literally of the manhood by itself, but as a conscious condescension of the divine-human Son.

The first kind of distinction comes to an end with the glorification of the Son. At that point, the condescension is reversed and he takes his rightful place at the Father's right hand. The second distinction, that of the spiritual and the physical, is radically modified. In the exaltation of the flesh of Christ is the exaltation of all of human nature.

# Chapter Five

# Conclusions

## Chrysostom's Interpretation of Christ

Christological definitions in the patristic period were born out of controversies alternately dealing with the deity of Christ, his humanity, and the relationship between the two natures in the incarnation. In the second and third centuries Gnostics like Marcion and Valentinus raised questions that resulted in the strong affirmation of the real humanity—or, at least, the real flesh—of Christ. The major issue of the fourth century was, because of the Arians' teaching, the deity of Christ. In the late fourth and early fifth century and beyond attention turned again to the humanity of Christ as Apollinaris and later authors proposed theories of the incarnation that either minimized the humanity or separated it from the divinity of Christ. These names and others—Sabellius, Marcellus, Paul of Samosata—frequently appear in the homilies of Chrysostom as landmarks of the debates in which orthodox Christians settled upon their most important affirmations.

When Chrysostom addressed Christians in two of the most important centers of Christianity in the East, Antioch and Constantinople, the general acceptance of Christ's full deity left theologians with the problem of reconciling that with his human nature. The Council of Constantinople of 381, which took place five years before Chrysostom began his writing and preaching, is, in its repetition and extension of Nicaean language, evidence of the decline of the Arian controversy and, in its condemnation of the ideas of Apollinaris, evidence too of the beginning of a new debate concentrating on the fullness of the humanity of Christ. After summarizing Chrysostom's views on the deity, humanity, and incarnation of Christ, we will turn to the question of his place in the "Antiochene" or "Alexandrian" schools.

The later phase of Neo-Arianism provided the occasion for Chrysostom to write and speak frequently on the full divinity of the Son. At an earlier period Arianism had dominated both Antioch and Constantinople. The preacher found himself in an ongoing debate with the Neo-Arians at a time when they had neither an ecclesiastical party nor the legal right to have their own congregations.

Chrysostom argued that the Neo-Arians' endless syllogisms— the method of argument preferred by Aëtius and continued by Eunomius and his followers—indicated the weakness of their position. Their over-confidence is most clearly seen, however, in their belief that they can define and know God's essence. The reason they may not say that the Son is unlike (ἀνόμοιος) the Father because he is essentially ungenerate while the Son is generate, is that they assume too much when they say they know that the Father's essence is ungeneratedness (ἀγέννησία). God's transcendence makes it possible to affirm the consubstantiality of the Father and the Son, without defining what their substance is.

Chrysostom further challenges the Anomoeans' exegesis. He explains texts that Arians had long used to show the disparity of being of the Son and the Father, such as: "The Son can do nothing of himself," and "I have come down from heaven not to do my own will, but the will of him who sent me" as statements of unity of being and purpose rather than distinctions of status. Nor does the fact that the Son is "sent" from the Father and is "given" things by the Father imply his inferiority, but simply indicate characteristics proper to Fatherhood and Sonship in contradistinction to the lack of distinctions found in Sabellianism. The same distinguishing of begetter and begotten is meant by "The Father is greater than I."

The orthodox have strong scriptural arguments of their own. Besides Christ's explicit statements such as "I and the Father are one," and "He who seems me sees also the Father," there are many occasions in which the Son's activities demonstrate the same power, honor, glory, worship, and authority as the Father's. All such evidence show the oneness of οὐσία of the two. If the Anomoeans are unsatisfied with such a theory which appeared to them to be that of simple dynamic oneness of the Ungenerate and the Begotten, that is only because they assume a more essential knowledge than what is given human beings to have.

In the end, like the Cappadocians, Chrysostom sees the *homoousion* of Nicaea as the key expression of the Son's full deity, and *hypostasis* as the category that distinguishes the Father from the Son, against theories like Sabellius' and Marcellus'. In the later decades of the fourth century, as in the earlier decades, the deity of the Son is still the most important point of theological contention.

Chrysostom is almost equally as emphatic with his congregations on the question of the Christ's humanity. The reality of the incarnation and its salvific effect depends upon the reality of the humanity that the Logos took. Many of Chrysostom's comments on the reality of Christ's humanity are directed against those who would conclude from such lowly depictions that Christ was less than God.

The ordinary functions of human nature include emotion, intellect and will. In his many homilies on the Gospels of Matthew and John, Chrysostom deals with such incidents as Jesus' weeping at the tomb of Lazarus, experiencing anxiety over his impending death, and suffering the agony in the garden. Such expressions of πάθος are real and attributable to the "human nature" of Christ or "our common nature." At a verbal level, Chrysostom thus differs from Apollinaris and his theological followers who used φύσις only in the singular (e.g., "one incarnate nature of the divine Logos"). But this human nature is not an independent and freely-acting center of consciousness in Christ. The divine nature completely predominates. Whenever there is an incident of human grief, or sorrow, or agony, it is a conscious demonstration of the reality of the humanity, but not an autonomous humanity. The closest Chrysostom comes to distinguishing the human operations of Christ from the Logos' operations is to describe the agony of the garden as a time when "he left his flesh deserted and stripped of any divine power of operation to show its weakness."[350]

Chrysostom seems little inclined to understand Christ's intellect as a human intellect. He explains any incidents of apparent ignorance in the gospels as didactic occasions. He assumes the incarnate Christ's omniscience just as easily as he assumes the Father's omniscience. Here the predominance of the Logos is clearer than in any other human function.

There are at least two occasions in which Chrysostom speaks of a duality of wills in Christ. While this may seem to point to an autonomous human nature, Chrysostom limits the distinction by associating the contrary will (in the agony of the garden) with the flesh.

The meaning of "flesh," σάρξ, is crucial to understanding Chrysostom's view of the Christ's humanity. It is the term he prefers above all others for this humanity. Some have argued that the term "flesh," as Chrysostom uses it, incorporates both the literal flesh and all the functions of a real human soul, and others that it includes only the body and its associated needs and simple reactions (the lower soul). The best characterization is the latter— that Chrysostom uses σάρξ most often in its primary corporeal sense, which includes the characteristics of the lower soul. In his exposition of Rom. 7 he describes the flesh as that which "is beneath the soul, as a harp beneath a harper, as a ship under the pilot."[351] His use of biblical terms like "temple" and "indwelling" refer likewise primarily to the real flesh of Christ.

Chrysostom's understanding, however, is not the same as Apollinaris.' He has no explicit theory of the divine Logos

---

[350] *De Incomprehensibili* 7, 6 (PG 48, 766).

[351] *Hom. in Rom.* 13 (Field 1, 101).

replacing the higher soul in Christ, which had been rejected by several synods and by the Council of Constantinople in 381. In at least two homilies Chrysostom explicitly rejects such a position. His sixth and seventh homilies on Philippians, preached in Constantinople, each affirm a human soul in Christ. But the brevity with which Chrysostom addresses the issue is perhaps just as significant. He says little more than making two direct comments: "For we indeed are soul and body, but he was God, and soul and body," and "If 'the form of God' is 'perfect God,' then the 'form of a servant' is 'a perfect servant.'"[352] One can only conclude that Apollinaris' ideas were not a widespread threat that required the protective teaching of the preacher and bishop of Antioch and Constantinople. The reason may be either that the discussion stayed in a comparatively small circle of disputants and was perceived to be adequately treated by the assemblies that addressed it, or that Chrysostom, like Athanasius before him, had no compelling theological reason to stress the complete human soul of Christ, or both.

Chrysostom's explanation of the incarnation goes beyond the simple language of confession, but has a definite boundary beyond which are realities that, he insists, are held only by faith. Historically, he shows awareness of the issues that would erupt into full controversy several decades after his death and uses some of the terms that those later theologians and ecclesiastical leaders used. The Council of Chalcedon will cite one of his statements on the relationship of the natures of Christ. But detailed discussions of the language of essence and natures do not dominate Chrysostom's teaching. Such terms are useful in explaining particularly difficult biblical texts, but Christology can best be described by elaborations upon the biblical language relating to God's great οἰκονομία.

It is the οἰκονομία itself that explains the relationship of the divine and human in Christ. Some experiences and characteristics

---

[352] *Hom. in Phil.* 8 (Field 5, 40).

that cannot be attributed to divinity itself, or to Christ according to his "pure nature," are properly attributed to Christ "according to the economy." This is the incarnate Christ, both Logos and flesh, about whom after the incarnation some things can be said that cannot be said before the incarnation. While οἰκονομία thus obviously involves the humanity with which the Logos was clothed, or which he "became," it is not usually a description of Christ's human nature considered apart from the divine nature.

The relationship of the two natures, of the Logos and the flesh, is one of unity and distinction. Their union is both ἕνωσις and συνάφεια, yet does not involve confusion: "By their union [ἑνώσει] and conjoining [συναφείᾳ], God, the Word, and the flesh are one, not as a result of commingling [συγχύσεως] or disappearance of substances [οὐσιῶν], but by some ineffable and inexplicable union [ἑνώσεως]." Chrysostom thus shows an awareness of the need to affirm both a real union and the duality of natures, but he does not try to qualify further the manner of the union as either hypostatic or prosopic. Perhaps he even anticipated the next stage of christological speculation and consciously limited his own definition to a ἕνωσις ineffable and inexplicable.

On numerous occasions Chrysostom distinguishes the human and the divine natures of Christ. But these texts must be interpreted carefully, for sometimes he is speaking of a distinction of "the pure nature" from "the economy," by which he means divine nature in itself, as distinct from the incarnate state of the Logos; and sometimes he is contrasting the characteristics of the flesh with those of divinity. In any case, the purpose of distinctions is never to posit a freely-acting assumed man who by being righteous and obedient demonstrated the possibility of the same righteousness in all human beings. On the contrary, the divine nature so dominates the humanity so that the relationship of the two can be described as an "unequal mixture of actions" and an "unequal union of natures."[353]

---

[353] *In quatrid. Lazarum* 1 (PG 50, 642-43).

The kinds of biblical passages that warrant distinguishing divinity and humanity are those that speak of Christ's identification with human experience (suffering, temptation), of any kind of change ("being made" or "anointed"), or of Christ's mediatorial roles (intercession, priesthood). Such biblical expressions must be taken seriously as real attributes of Christ. And they must describe something other than divinity itself, for the divine nature is immutable. They must describe Christ "according to the economy."

Condescension, a term Chrysostom uses often, explains the motive, the activity, and the appearance of Christ's incarnation. As early as Origen the concept had both apologetic and theological applications. Most importantly, it was the way Christians could affirm both God's transcendence and his involvement in the world. Chrysostom defines συγκατάβασις in this way: "God condescends whenever he is not seen as he is, but in the way one incapable of beholding him is able to look upon him."[354] In other words, the vast difference between the Creator and the creature means that human knowledge of the divine will always be limited to an accommodated revelation. The greatest example of condescension is the incarnation itself. Nearly all of Christ's lowly, human activities and attributes are to be understood as condescension. Thus God reveals himself in forms that teach, but by analogy. Ordinary human limitations attributed to Christ (for example: ignorance, temptation, and such) are not the characteristics of a human nature distinct and isolated; rather, they are the self-conscious revelations of the divine and human Christ who was providing a detailed model of what human behavior can and should be. The one human characteristic of Christ that is not a condescension is his flesh, which is to be understood as literal corporeality.

---

[354] *De Incomprehensibili* 3, 163-66 (Malingrey, p. 200).

## Chrysostom's Place in Emerging Christologies

The literature on Chrysostom's theology inevitably raises the question of his relationship to Antiochene theological trends, or the so-called "Antiochene school." While some have seen him as a classic example of Antiochene theology, others have questioned that opinion and have, in fact, placed Chrysostom closer to the Alexandrian approach. The texts studied here show that Chrysostom's Christology contains elements of both approaches, and thus he is not a classic example of either. While we find a methodology that is clearly similar to that of Theodore of Mopsuestia and other Antiochene exegetes and theologians, Chrysostom's theological foundations most often reflect those of Athanasius and of later Alexandrians. It might be helpful to summarize at this point some of the specific characteristics of both approaches in Chrysostom's thought.

The theological characteristics of what has been called the Antiochene school are to be found primarily in Theodore of Mopsuestia, Chrysostom's contemporary and fellow-student, and in Nestorius, his eventual successor in the see of Constantinople. The position is usually described as more Aristotelian, and consequently more likely to view Christ's humanity in concrete terms. His was a full human life, possessing all the properties and functions that any other human being had, including all the operations of the higher, rational, soul. His earthly life resulted in a moral and ethical victory that provides the model for all subsequent human struggles with, and victories over, sin. The full and distinct human life of Christ—the assumed Man—is thus essential. Unless a real man accomplished moral and spiritual victory, there is nothing concrete that can be offered to the rest of the human race.

Chrysostom has some of the same exegetical approaches as other Antiochenes. His interest is in the historical meaning of the text; and in his systematic and detailed writing and preaching on so many of the books of the Bible he rarely ignores the kind of difficult text that describes Christ in "lowly ways." Consequently, there are many occasions on which he distinguishes the human and divine in Christ. In the gospels that includes occasions of anguish, suffering, and temptation, and, in the book of Hebrews, roles of mediation and identification with human weakness.

Probably a clearer parallel between Chrysostom and other Antiochenes is the moralism of his preaching. Christ appears as the exemplar of Christian obedience, endurance in suffering, and resistance in the face of temptation. Thus: "The actions performed by Christ in a human way were so performed not merely for the purpose of confirming the incarnation, but also that he might instruct us to virtuous living."[355] However, two qualifications must be made on this important point. First, the literature that we are dealing with is homilies or homiletic commentaries, which by its very nature is oriented toward exhortation. Second, although Chrysostom often says that Christ provided a model for human behavior, he does not describe Christ's human life as a personal moral victory that provides the foundation of salvation for the rest of mankind. Christ's humanity may be a picture of, but is not necessarily an experiment in, human obedience. This is neither more nor less docetic than the understanding of Athanasius and other theologians of the fourth century who admitted the reality of the humanity of Christ in principle and saw its expression mostly in the characteristics of flesh and its attendant needs and responses, but who looked at the obedience of Christ as demonstration. This is what Chrysostom means by condescension. In Christ, God was revealing many things that cannot be taken in their normal, literal, sense. The flesh of Christ was literally real, and should not be taken as a condescension, but many other pictures of Christ "according to the economy" are accommodations to human comprehension.

"Alexandrian" Christology is usually described as more mystical and Platonic than its counterpart. The corruption of the

---

[355] *Hom. in Jn.* 49, 1 (PG 59, 273).

human race is more likely to be seen as a great decline into non-being, rather than individual moral failure. Humanity is conceived of as an ontological whole, and thus the incarnation of Christ is his being clothed with the whole of humanity. The incarnation itself is salvific for in it humanity is truly united to divinity, which divinizes the lower nature. There remain not two natures, but one. To keep the human and divine natures distinct at this point is, to the Alexandrian way of thinking, to undermine the very means by which human nature is saved. Christ is one person with one determining nature.

While Chrysostom is not inclined to define sin, human nature, and Christ in ontological language, he nonetheless views the incarnation as the real and permanent union of two natures that itself is the salvation of the human race. If this soteriological principle is not as predominant in Chrysostom as it is in Athanasius, that is because Chrysostom simultaneously holds other models of salvation like substitutionary sacrifice and human faith. Interspersed throughout his homilies are the ideas of divinization, the *communicatio idiomatum*, and the elevation of human nature in the heavenly session of Christ.

The "Alexandrian" tendencies in Chrysostom's theology are more apparent, however, in his descriptions of Christ himself. There is no attempt to depict a human intellect or the human volitional capability to choose rightly and thereby merit salvation. On the contrary, there is a singular subject of Christ's actions, the Logos, who determines every rational and volitional experience in the incarnation. Chrysostom regularly uses "nature" in the singular. The one set of functions that is different is that which is more closely associated with the flesh itself: fear, agony, suffering, and grief. This belongs to the "humanity" which is clearly distinguishable, but only because of the axiomatic contrast of spirit and flesh. The "temple" or "clothing" of Christ is his flesh, not the assumed Man as the Antiochenes would have it. In this Chrysostom is very similar to Athanasius, Cyril, and others who maintain a real unity while distinguishing the characteristics of the flesh.

Chrysostom is "Antiochene" to the extent that he depends predominantly on the biblical text to provide the theological language that will enable him to describe the person of Christ and the nature of the incarnation insofar as that is possible. He is "Alexandrian" to the extent that he portrays Christ as one divine acting subject whose actions are human-like because he is portraying human functions by a conscious condescension of his own nature, or, in some instances, actually human because he is showing the real nature of the literal flesh which he united to himself in the incarnation.

## Further Questions

This study has at least touched on several major theological topics besides Christology including soteriology and anthropology; and on several key questions in the history of theology in the fourth century, for instance, the relationship of different theological schools and the influence of controversies like Neo-Arianism and Apollinarianism. We conclude by raising some of the questions which are consequences of the present study but which could not be pursued here.

The contrast of the two Christologies of the Antiochene and Alexandrian schools obviously has bearing on any study of Chrysostom's thought, and past studies show a great interest in the question. The conclusion here is that Chrysostom presents something of a composite of emphases of both sides. The resulting question will be: why does the individual not fit the scheme? But it will be just as valid to ask: does the scheme fit the data? Many studies of patristic Christologies have in recent years asked whether this or that figure belongs more properly in the line of thought of Antioch or Alexandria. While it is not the purpose of this study to either endorse or reject the traditional scheme, a task that would necessarily involve the analysis of all major thinkers of the period, we must conclude that Chrysostom does more to detract from it than to reinforce it.

The recent interest in Arianism and Neo-Arianism has resulted in a more detailed analysis not just of their philosophical presuppositions, but also of their theological, exegetical, and ethical understandings. Chrysostom provides a perspective on the Neo-Arians somewhat different than, and complementary to, the picture we get from the treatises of Gregory of Nazianzus and Basil of Caesarea against the leading Neo-Arian, Eunomius. It is clear in Chrysostom's homilies that Neo-Arianism continued to be influential in the late fourth century. This raises the question of the relationship of the Arian controversy and the christological controversy. To what extent are the early formulations of the humanity of Christ from the mid-fourth century on still a reaction against the teachings of Arius and his successors?

On the other hand, what are we to make of the relative disinterest in the ideas of Apollinaris? Synods in Rome, Alexandria, and Antioch, and the Council of Constantinople, were interested enough to condemn his ideas, but why would the particulars of his theory not appear more than once or twice in hundreds of homilies preached in the important cities of Antioch and Constantinople? The way Arius opened the issue of the divine status of the Son is clearly different from how Apollinaris approached the question of Christ's humanity.

Chrysostom reflects at many points the same understanding that Athanasius had of the natures of Christ and of the incarnation. Is this because Athanasius' thought was so influential in the late fourth century? Or is it because he, and Chrysostom, and for that matter Apollinaris and Cyril, reflect a prevailing assumption in the East that Christ is one divine acting subject? And does this further cast the ideas of Theodore of Mopsuestia and Nestorius in the role of a distinct minority?

All of Chrysostom's theology is exegetical in nature. Recent studies of the history of exegesis have aroused interest in the relationship of exegesis and speculative theology. Chrysostom's materials are an excellent source for the study of exegesis and of the relationship between exegesis and theology in the fourth-century East.

Finally, there is the question of the relationship of Christology and other theological themes. For instance, Chrysostom's Christology raises questions about the soteriologies of his period. How many major models of salvation are there in the fourth century? What are their sources? Chrysostom, among others, seems to hold several different models simultaneously. How do these varied themes relate to each other? And how determinative are soteriological theories in shaping Christology? Further studies of Chrysostom's theology could widen our picture of the converging influences of exegesis, philosophy, theology, and pastoral theology in the Greek patristic world.[356]

I hope that this study has clarified what has been in the past a somewhat confusing picture of John Chrysostom's Christology. This prolific writer and orator of the ancient East is best understood when some of the traditional categories of the history of doctrines are set aside. Viewed apart from these categories, the theology contained in his hundreds of homilies and homiletical commentaries includes a Christology that in fact resembles the definition of Chalcedon in its fundamental assertions. Removing Chrysostom from his traditional place alongside Diodore, Theodore and Nestorius further isolates and limits the so-called "Word-man" Christology; but that, in the end, results in a better understanding of what was predominant in early assumptions about Christ, his incarnation, and its salvific effects.

---

[356] Robert Carter has suggested further theological investigations as a priority in Chrysostom studies second only to the production of critical editions. "The Future of Chrysostom Studies: Theology and Nachleben," in Christou, ΣΥΜΠΟΣΙΟΝ, pp. 129-36.

# Selected Bibliography

## Sources

Chrysostom, John. *A Théodore*. Edited and translated by Jean Dumortier. SC, 117. Paris: Les Éditions du cerf, 1966.

_____. *A une jeune veuve. Sur le mariage unique*. Edited by Gerard H. Ettlinger. Fr. Trans. by Bernard Grillet. SC, 138. Paris: Les Éditions du cerf, 1968.

_____. *Baptismal Instructions*. Translated by Paul W. Harkins. ACW, 31. Westminster, Md., 1963.

_____. *Commentaire sur Isaïe*. Edited by Jean Dumortier. SC, 304. Paris: Les Éditions du cerf, 1983.

_____. *Commentary on Saint John: Homilies 1-47*. Translated by T. A. Goggin. FC, 33. New York: The Fathers of the Church, 1957.

_____. *Commentary on Saint John: Homilies 48-88*. Translated by T. A. Goggin. FC, 41. New York: The Fathers of the Church, 1960.

_____. *Demonstration Against the Pagans that Christ is God*. Translated by Paul Harkins. FC, 73. Washington, D. C.: Catholic U. of America, 1985.

_____. *Discourse on Blessed Babylas and Against the Greeks*. Translated by M. Schatkin. FC, 73. Washington, D. C.: Catholic U. of America, 1985.

_____. *Discourses Against Judaizing Christians*. Translated by Paul W. Harkins. FC, 68. Washington, D. C.: Catholic U. of America Press, 1979.

_____. *Exhortations a Théodore; Lettres à Olympias*. Translated by Ph.-E. Legrand. Paris: Gabalda, 1933.

_____. *Huit catéchèses batismales inédites*. Edited and translated by A. Wenger. SC, 50. Paris: Les Éditions du cerf, 1957.

_____. *In Praise of St. Paul*. Translated by Th. Halton. Boston: Daughters of St. Paul, 1963.

_____. *Lettres à Olympias*. Edited and translated by A.-M. Malingrey. SC, 13. Paris: Les Éditions du cerf, 1947.

_____. *Lettre d'exile à Olympias et a tous les Fidèles*. Edited and translated by A.-M. Malingrey. SC, 103. Paris: Les Éditions du cerf, 1964.

_____. *On the Incomprehensible Nature of God*. Translated by Paul W. Harkins, FC, vol. 72 (1984).

_____. *Panégyriques de Saint Paul*. Edited by Auguste Piédagnel. SC, 300. Paris: Les Éditions du cerf, 1982.

_____. *The Priesthood*. Translated by W. A. Jurgens. New York: Macmillan, 1955.

_____. *S. Iohannis Chrysostomi opera omnia*. Edited by Bernard de Montfaucon. 12 vols. Paris, 1718-38 and Venice, 1734-41. Reprinted by Migne, J. P., ed. *Patrologiae Cursus Completus, Series Graeca*. Vols. 47-64. Paris: 1863-64.

_____. *S. Iohannis Chrysostomi opera omnia*. Edited by Henry Savile. 8 vols. Eton, 1612.

_____. *Sancti Patris Nostri Joannis Chrysostomi archiepiscopi Constantinopolitani Interpretatio omnium epistularum Paulinarum per homilias facta*. Edited by Frederick Field. 7 vols. Oxford: Bibliotheca Patrum Ecclesiae Catholicae, 1849-62.

_____. *Sur la providence de Dieu*. Edited and translated by A.-M. Malingrey. SC, 79. Paris: Les Éditions du cerf, 1961.

_____. *Sur la vaine gloire et l'education des enfants*. Edited and translated by A.-M. Malingrey. SC, 13. Paris: Les Éditions du cerf, 1947.

_____. *Sur l'egalite du Pere et du Fils: Contre les anomeens, homilies VII-XII*. Edited and translated by A.-M. Malingrey. Paris: Les Éditions du cerf, 1994.

_____. *Sur l'incomprehensibilité de Dieu: Tome 1 (Homilies I-V)*. 2nd ed. Edited by A.-M. Malingrey. Translated by R. Flacelière. SC, 13. Paris: Les Éditions du cerf, 1947.

_____. *Sur le sacerdoce; dialogue et homelie*. Edited and translated by A.-M. Malingrey. Paris: Les Éditions du cerf, 1980.

_____. *La virginité*. Edited by H. Musurillo. Translated by B. Grillet. SC, 125. Paris: Les Éditions du cerf, 1966.

_____. *Works*. In Philip Schaff, ed. *A Select Library of the Nicene and Post-Nicene Fathers*, vols. 9-14. Buffalo and New York, 1889; reprint ed., Grand Rapids, Mich.: Wm. B. Eerdmans, 1975.

Palladius, Bishop of Aspuna. *Dialogue sur la vie de Jean Chrysostome*. Edited and and translated by A.-M. Malingrey. Paris: Les Éditions du cerf, 1988.

## Literature

Aldama, J. A. de., ed. *Repertorium pseudochrysostomicum*. Paris: Centre national de la recherche scientifique, 1965.

Altaner, Berthold. *Patrology*. Translated by H. C. Graef. Freiburg: Herder, 1960.

Amand De Mendieta, Emmanuel. "L'incompréhensibilité de l'Essence divine d'après Jean Chrysostome." In ΣΥΜΠΟΣΙΟΝ, pp. 23-40.

Attwater, Donald. *St. John Chrysostom: The Voice of Gold*. Milwaukee: Bruce, 1939.

Aubineau, Michel, ed. *Codices Chrysostomici Graeci I: Britanniae et Hiberniae*. Paris: Centre national de la recherche scientifique, 1968.

Aubineau, Michel. "Les homélies pascales de Saint Jean Chrysostome." In *ΣΥΜΠΟΣΙΟΝ: Studies on St. John Chrysostom*. Edited by P. Christou. Thessaloniki: Patriarchal Institute for Patristic Studies, 1973.

Bardy, G. "St Jean Chrysostome." *Dictionnaire de Théologie Catholique* 8:1, pp. 660-90.

_____. "'Philosophie' et 'Philosophe' dans le vocabulaire chrétien des premiers siècles." *Revue d'ascétique et de mystique* 25 (1949): 97-108.

Barnard, L. R. "Christology and Soteriology in the Preaching of John Chrysostom." Dissertation, Southwestern Baptist Theological Seminary, 1974.

Bartelink, G. J. M. "'Philosophie' et 'Philosophe' dans quelques oeuvres de Jean Chrysostome." *Revue d'ascétique et de mystique* 144 (1960): 486-92.

Baur, Chrysostomus. *John Chrysostom and His Time*. Vol. 1: *Antioch*; Vol. 2: *Constantinople*. Translated by Sr. M. Gonzaga. Westminster, Md.: Newman, 1959-60.

_____. *S. Jean Chrysostome et ses oeuvres dans l'histoire littéraire*. Recueil des travaux publiés par les membres des conférences d'histoire et de philologie, vol. 18. Louvain and Paris: Université de Louvain, 1907.

Benin, Stephen D. "Sacrifice as Education in Augustine and Chrysostom (Divine Accomodation in History)." *Church History* 52 (1983): 7-20.

Bobrinskoy, Boris. "The Indwelling of the Spirit in Christ: 'Pneumatic Christology' in the Cappadocian Fathers." *St. Vladimir's Theological Quarterly* 28,1 (1984): 49-65.

Brandle, Rudolf. "Jean Chrysostome: l'importance de Matth 25:31-46 pour son éthique." *Vig Chr* 31, 1 (1977): 47-52.

_____. *Matth. 25, 31-46 im Werk des Johannes Chrysostomos: Ein Beitrag zur Auslegungsgeschichte und zur Erforschung der Ethik der griechischen Kirche um die Wende vom 4. zum 5. Jahrhundert*. Tübingen: Mohr, 1979.

Burger, Douglas C. *A Complete Bibliography of the Scholarship on the Life and Works of Saint John Chrysostom*. Evanston, Ill.: By the Author, 1964.

Bush, R. W. *The Life and Times of Chrysostom*. London, 1885.

Campenhausen, Hans von. "John Chrysostom." In *The Fathers of the Greek Church*, pp. 140-57. Translated by L. A. Garrard. London: Black, 1963.

Carter, Robert. "The Chronology of St. John Chrysostom's Early Life." *Traditio* 18 (1962): 357-64.

_____., ed. *Codices Chrysostomici Graeci II: Germaniae*. Paris: Center national de la recherche scientifique, 1970.

_____., ed. *Codices Chrysostomici Graeci III: Americae et Europae Occidentalis*. Paris: Center national de la recherche scientifique, 1970.

_____. "The Future of Chrysostom Studies: Theology and Nachleben" In *ΣΥΜΠΟΣΙΟΝ*, pp. 129-36.

Chadwick, Henry. "Eucharist and Christology in the Nestorian Controversy." *J Th St* N.S. 2 (1951): 145-64.

Chase, F. H. *Chrysostom, a Study in the History of Biblical Interpretation.* Cambridge, 1887.

Clark, Elizabeth A. *Jerome, Chrysostom, and Friends: Essays and Translations. Studies in Women and Religion.* Vol. 1. New York and Toronto: Edwin Mellen, 1979.

Coleman-Norton, P. R. *Palladii Dialogus de Vita Sancti Johannis Chrysostomi.* Cambridge, Mass.: Harvard U. Press, 1928.

_____. "St. Chrysostom and the Greek Philosophers." *Classical Philology* 25 (1930): 305-07.

Coman, Jean. "Le rapport de la justification et de la charité dans les homélies de Saint Jean Chrysostome à l'Épître aux Romains." *Studia Evangelica* 5 (1968): 248-71.

_____. "L'unité du genre humain d'apres saint Jean Chrysostome." In *ΣΥΜΠΟΣΙΟΝ*, pp. 41-58.

Courcelle, P. "L'âme en cage." In *Parusia. Festg. J. Hirschberger*, pp. 103-16. Frankfurt, 1965.

Daniélou, Jean. "L'incompréhensibilité de Dieu d'après saint Jean Chrysostome." *Recherches de science religieuse* 37 (1950): 176-94.

Dewart, Joanne. "The Notion of 'Person' Underlying the Christology of Theodore of Mopsuestia." *Stud Patr* 12 (1975): 199-207.

Diekamp, Franz. *Doctrina Patrum de Incarnatione Verbi: ein griechisches Florilegium aus der Wende des siebenten und achten Jahrhunderts.* Münster, 1907.

Diepen, H. M. "L'Assumptus homo à Chalcédoine." *Revue Thomiste* 50 (1951).

Downey, Glanville. *A History of Antioch in Syria.* Princeton: Princeton U. Press, 1961.

Dragas, G. D. "St. John Chrysostom's Doctrine of God's Providence." *Ekklesiastikos Pharos* 57 (1975): 375-406.

Dreyfus, François. "Divine Condescendence (synkatabasis) as a Hermeneutic Principle of the Old Testament in Jewish and Christian Tradition." Translated by L. Dempsey. *Immanuel* 19 (1984-85): 74-86.

Duchatelez, K. "La «condescendance» divine et l'histoire du salut." *Nouvelle revue théologique* 95 (1973): 593-621.

Dumortier, J. "La culture profane de S. Jean Chrysostome." *Mélanges de science religieuse* 10 (1953): 53-62.

_____. "Les idées morales de Jean Chrysostome." *Mélanges de science religieuse* 12 (1955): 27-36.

_____. "La valeur historique du dialogue de Palladius et la chronologie de saint Jean Chrysostome." *Mélanges de science religieuse* 7 (1951): 51-56.

Elser, Dr. "Der hl. Chrysostomus und die Philosophie." *Theologische Quartalschrift* 76 (1864): 550-76.

Festugière, A. J. *Antioche paienne et chrétienne: Libanius, Chrysostome et les moines de Syrie.* Paris: E. de Boccard, 1959.

Foerster, Th. *Chrysostomus in seinem Verhältniss zur antiochenischen Schule: Ein Beitrag zur Dogmengeschichte.* Gotha, 1869.

Galtier, P. S. "Athanase et l'âme humaine du Christ." *Gregorianum* 36 (1955): 553-89.

Garrett, Duane A. *An Analysis of the Hermeneutics of John Chrysostom's Commentary on Isaiah 1-8 with an English Translation.* Lewiston: E. Mellen Press, 1992.

Gesché, A. "L'âme humaine de Jesus dans la Christologie du IVe siècle." *Revue d'histoire ecclésiastique* 54 (1959): 385-90, 403-09.

Grandsire, A. "Nature et hypostasis dans saint Basile." *Recherches des science religieuse* 13 (1923): 130-52.

Greer, R. A. The Analogy of Grace in Theodore of Mopsuestia's Christology. *J Th St* N.S. 34 (1983): 82-98.

_____. "The Antiochene Christology of Diodore of Tarsus." *J Th St* N.S. 17 (1966): 327-41.

_____. *The Captain of our Salvation: A Study in the Patristic Exegesis of Hebrews.* Tübingen, 1973.

_____. *Theodore of Mopsuestia: Exegete and Theologian.* London, 1961.

_____. "The Use of Scripture in the Nestorian Controversy." *Scot J Th* 20 (1967): 413-422.

Gregg, R.C. and Groh, D.E. *Early Arianism—A View of Salvation.* Philadelphia: Fortress, 1981.

Grillmeier, Alois. *Christ in Christian Tradition: From the Apostolic Age to Chalcedon (451).* 2nd ed. Translated by J. S. Bowden. Atlanta: John Knox, 1975.

Haidacher, S. *Die Lehre des heiligen Johannes Chrysostomus über die Schriftinspiration.* Salzburg, 1897.

Halkin, François. *Douze récits byzantins sur saint Jean Chrysostome.* Subsidia Hagiographica, 60. Brussels: Société des Bollandistes, 1977.

Halleux, A. de "'Hypostase' et 'Personne' dans la formation du dogme trinitaire (ca 375-381)." *Revue d'histoire ecclésiastique* 79 (1984): 313-69.

Hanson, R. P. C. "The Doctrine of the Trinity Achieved in 381." *Scot J Th* 36 (1983): 41-57.

_____. *The Search for the Christian Doctrine of God: the Arian Controversy 318-381.* Edinburgh, T & T Clark, 1988.

Hardy, Edward R. *Christology of the Later Fathers.* The Library of Christian Classics. Philadelphia: Westminster, 1954.

Harkins, Paul. "Chrysostom the Apologist: On the Divinity of Christ." In *Kyriakon: Festschrift Johannes Quasten,* vol. 2, pp. 441-51. Edited by P. Granfield and J. A. Jungmann. Münster Westf.: Aschendorff, 1970.

_____. "John Chrysostom." *New Catholic Encyclopedia* 7:1041-44.

Hill, Robert. "Akribeia: A Principle of Chrysostom's Exegesis." *Colloquium* 14 (1981): 32-36.

_____. "St. John Chrysostom's Teaching on Inspiration in Six Homilies on Isaiah." *Vig Chr* 22 (April 1968): 19-37.

Hoffmann-Aleith, E. "Das Paulusverständnis des Johannes Chrysostomus." *Zeitschrift für die neutestamentliche Wissenschaft* 38 (1939): 181-88.

Hubbell, H. M. "Chrysostom and Rhetoric." *Classical Philology* 18 (1924): 261-76.

Jones, A. H. M. "St. John Chrysostom's Parentage and Education." *Harv Th R* 46 (1953): 171-73.

Juzek, J. H. *Die Christologie des hl. Joh. Chrysostomus: Zugleich ein Beitrag zur Dogmatik der Antiochener.* Breslau, 1912.

Kaczynski, Reiner. *Das Wort Gottes in Liturgie und Alltag der Gemeinden des Johannes Chrysostomus.* Freiburger Theologische Studien, vol. 94. Freiburg im Breisgau: Herder, 1974.

Kannengiesser, Charles. "Arius and the Arians." *Th St* 44 (1983): 456-75.

_____. "Athanasius of Alexandria and the Foundation of Traditional Christology." *Th St* 34 (1973): 103-13.

_____. "The Athanasian Decade 1974-84: A Bibliographical Report." *Th St* 46 (1985): 524-41.

_____. *Holy Scripture and Hellenistic Hermeneutics in Alexandrian Christology: the Arian Crisis.* Berkeley: The Center for Hermeneutical Studies, 1982.

_____., ed. *Jean Chrysostome et Augustin: actes du colloque de Chantilly, 22-24 Septembre 1974.* Théologie historique, 35. Paris: Éditions Beauchesne, 1975.

_____. "Une nouvelle interprétation de la christologie d'Apollinaire." *Revue des sciences religieuses* 59 (1971): 27-36.

Kelly, J. N. D. *Early Christian Doctrines.* 5th ed. New York: Harper and Row, 1976.

_____. *Golden Mouth: The Story of John Chrysostom: Ascetic, Preacher, Bishop.* London: Duckworth, 1995.

Kenny, A. "Was St. John Chrysostom a Semi-Pelagian?" *Irish Theological Quarterly* 27 (1960): 16-29.

Kopecek, Thomas A. *A History of Neo-Arianism.* 2 vols. Patristic Monograph Series, 8. Philadelphia: Philadelphia Patristic Foundation, 1979.

Korbacher, J. *Ausserhalb der Kirche kein Heil? Eine dogmengeschichtliche Untersuchung über Kirche und Kirchenzugehörigkeit bei Johannes Chrysostomus.* Münchener Theologische Studien, 27. Munich: Hueber, 1963.

Krupp, R. A. *Saint John Chrysostom: A Scripture Index.* Lanham, Md.: University of America Press, 1984.

Laistner, M. L. *Christianity and Pagan Culture in the Later Roman Empire together with an English Translation of John Chrysostom's "Address on Vainglory and the Right Way for Parents to Bring up their Children."* Ithaca, N.Y.: Cornell U. Press, 1951.

Lecuyer, J. "Le sacerdoce céleste du Christ selon Chrysostome." *Nouvelle revue théologique* 72 (1950): 561-79.

Leroux, Jean-Marie. "Jean Chrysostome et la querelle origéniste." In *Epektasis: Mélanges Jean Dainélou*, pp. 335-41. Edited by J. Fontaine and Ch. Kannengiesser.

Liebeschuetz, J. H. W. G. *Barbarians and Bishops: Army, Church, and State in the Age of Arcadius and Chrysostom*. Oxford: Clarendon Press, 1990.

Lietzmann, H. *Apollinaris von Laodicea und seine Schule*. Tübingen: J. C. B. Mohr, 1904.

Malingrey, A.-M. *Indices Chrysostomici I: Ad Olympiadem; Ab Exilio Epistula; De Providentia Dei*. Hildesheim and New York: George Olms, 1978.

_____. *La litterature grecque chretienne*. Paris, Cerf, 1996.

McKenzie, J. L. "Annotations on the Christology of Theodore of Mopsuestia." *Th St* 19 (1958): 345-73.

Meeks, W. A. and Wilken, R. L. *Jews and Christians in Antioch in the First Four Centuries of the Common Era*. Society of Biblical Literature Sources for Biblical Study, no. 13. Missoula, Montana: Scholars Press, 1978.

Michaud, E. "La christologie de St. Jean Chrysostome." *Revue internationale de théologie* 17 (1909): 275-91.

_____. "La sotériologie de St. Jean Chrysostome." *Revue internationale de théologie* 18 (1910): 35-49.

Naegele, A. "Johannes Chrysostomos und sein Verhältnis zum Hellenismus." *Byzantinische Zeitschrift* 13 (1904): 73-113.

Neander, J. A. W. *The Life of St. Chrysostom*. Translated by J. C. Stapleton. 2 Vols. London, 1845.

Norris, Richard A., ed. *The Christological Controversy*. Sources of Early Christian Thought. Philadelphia: Fortress, 1980.

_____. *Manhood and Christ: A Study in the Christology of Theodore of Mopsuestia*. Oxford and New York, 1963.

Pelikan, Jaroslav. *The Christian Tradition. Vol. 1: The Emergence of the Catholic Tradition*. Chicago: University of Chicago Press, 1971.

Puech, Aimé. *Saint John Chrysostom*. Translated by M. Partridge. London: Duckworth, 1902.

Pinard, H. "Les infiltrations païennes dans l'ancienne loi d'après les pères de l'Église. La thèse de la condescendance." *Recherches des science religieuse* 9 (1919): 197-221.

Pollard, T. E. *Johannine Christology and the Early Church*. Cambridge and New York, 1970.

Prestige, G. L. *God in Patristic Thought*. 2nd ed. London: S.P.C.K., 1952.

Quasten, Johannes. *Patrology III: The Golden Age of Greek Patristic Literature from the Council of Nicaea to the Council of Chalcedon*. Westminster, Md.: Newman, 1963.

Raven, C. E. *Apollinarianism*. Cambridge and New York, 1923.

Richard, M. S. "Athanase et la psychologie du Christ selon les Ariens." *Mélanges de science religieuse* 4 (1947): 5-54.

Riedmatten, H. de. "Some Neglected Aspects of Apollinarist Christology." *Dominican Studies* 1 (1948): 239-60.

Roldanus, J. *Le Christ et l'homme dans la théologie d'Athanase d'Alexandrie. Étude de la conjonction de sa conception de l'homme avec sa christologie.* 2nd ed. Leiden: E.J. Brill, 1977.

Rusch, William G., ed. *The Trinitarian Controversy.* Sources of Early Christian Thought. Philadelphia: Fortress, 1980.

Sellers, R. V. *The Council of Chalcedon.* London, 1953.

_____. *Two Ancient Christologies.* London and New York: S.P.C.K., 1940.

Sieben, Hermann Joseph. *Voces: Eine Bibliographie zu Wörtern und Begriffen aus der Patristik (1918-1978).* Berlin and New York: Walter de Gruyter, 1980.

Simonetti, Manlio. *Biblical Interpretation in the Early Church: an Historical Introduction to Patristic Exegesis.* Translated by John A. Hughes. Edinburgh: T & T Clark, 1994.

Stephens, W. R. W. *Saint John Chrysostom: His Life and Times.* London: Murray, 1872.

Sullivan, F. A. *The Christology of Theodore of Mopsuestia.* Rome, 1956.

_____. "Further Notes on Theodore of Mopsuestia: a Reply to Fr. McKenzie." *Th St* 20 (1959): 264-79.

Telfer, Wm. "The Fourth Century Greek Fathers as Exegetes." *Harv Th R* 50 (1957): 91-105.

Tetz, M. "Das kritische Word vom Kreuz und die Christologie bei Athanasius von Alexandrien." In *Theologia crucis, signum crucis. Festschrift für Erich Dinkler,* pp. 447-65, 1979.

Thonnard, F.-J. "Saint Jean Chrysostome et saint Augustin dans la controverse pélagienne." *Revue des Études Byzantines* 25 (1967): 189-218.

Wallace-Hadrill, D. S. *Christian Antioch: A Study of Early Christian Thought in the East.* Cambridge: Cambridge U. Press, 1982.

_____. *The Greek Patristic View of Nature.* New York: Barnes & Noble, 1968.

Weigl, Eduard. *Christologie vom Tode des Athanasius bis zum Ausbruch des Nestorianischen Streites (373-429).* Münchener Studien zur historischen Theologie, 4. Munich, 1925.

Wenger, A. "La tradition des oeuvres de saint Jean Chrysostome I. Catéchèses inconnues et homélies peu connues." *Revue des Études Byzantines* 14 (1956): 5-47.

Wiles, M. F. "The Doctrine of Christ in the Patristic Age." In *Christ for us Today.* Edited by N. Pittenger, 1968.

Wilken, Robert L. *John Chrysostom and the Jews: Rhetoric and Reality in the Late Fourth Century.* Berkeley: University of California Press, 1983.

_____. "Tradition, Exegesis and the Christological Controversy." *Church History* 34 (1965): 123-42.

Winslow, D. F. "Christology and Exegesis in the Cappadocians." *Church History* 40 (1971): 389-96.

Winslow, D. F. *The Dynamics of Salvation*. Cambridge, Mass., 1979.

Young, Frances M. "Christological Ideas in the Greek Commentaries on the Epistle to the Hebrews." *J Th St* N.S. 20 (1969): 150-63.

_____. "A Reconsideration of Alexandrian Christology." *J Eccl H* 22 (1971): 103-14.

_____. *The Use of Sacrificial Ideas in Greek Christian Writers from the New Testament to John Chrysostom*. Patristic Monograph Series, no. 5. Philadelphia, 1979.

Zitnik, M. "Das Sein des Menschen zu Gott nach Johannes Chrysostomus." *Orientalia Christiana Periodica* 42 (1976): 368-401.

Zitnik, M. "Θεὸς φιλάνθρωπο" bei Johannes Chrysostomus." *Orientalia Christiana Periodica* 41 (1976): 76-118.